POLICE

CRIME

PREVENTION

POLICE

CRIME

PREVENTION

By

V. A. LEONARD, B.S., M.A., Ph.D.

CHARLES C THOMAS • PUBLISHER

Springfield • *Illinois* • *U.S.A.*

Published and Distributed Throughout the World by
CHARLES C THOMAS • PUBLISHER
Bannerstone House
301-327 East Lawrence Avenue, Springfield, Illinois, U.S.A.
Natchez Plantation House
735 North Atlantic Boulevard, Fort Lauderdale, Florida, U.S.A.

© *1972 by* CHARLES C THOMAS • PUBLISHER
ISBN 0-398-02339-5
Library of Congress Catalog Card Number: 70-169884

With THOMAS BOOKS *careful attention is given to all details of
manufacturing and design. It is the Publisher's desire to present books
that are satisfactory as to their physical qualities and artistic possibilities
and appropriate for their particular use.* THOMAS BOOKS *will be true
to those laws of quality that assure a good name and good will.*

HV
8031
L44

Printed in the United States of America
X-2

PREFACE

THIS BOOK is concerned with the problems of delinquency and crime in the smaller cities and communities of the nation. It portrays the futility of depending upon enforcement alone and draws the blueprints for a delinquency and crime prevention program designed to be both feasible and practical in police departments with a personnel strength of from one to seventy-five officers. It is in the smaller cities and communities that a very large segment of police service in this country is delivered.

Human behavior is the most overwhelming fact of life. It has been and is today humanity's chief concern all the way from the rostrum of the United Nations to the second grade classroom and the child guidance clinic. The shaper of man's destiny, it seems to have challenged any attempt to understand it or control it. Yet as will be seen in the pages to come, there are brilliant lights on the horizon which illuminate the way toward significant developments in the months and years ahead.

In the long struggle of mankind for self-control, human behavior has played a major role in the generation of social problems that plague an organized society. Foremost on this list of social liabilities is the problem of crime and the criminal which poses a threat to every man, woman and child in this country. The nature and extent of delinquency and crime in the United States, and its cost, are outlined in Chapter 1, and it clearly indicates the need for strong measures in every city, community and rural area across the nation.

The notion that crime was primarily a problem of the larger cities has long since been abandoned. Freeways, major arterials, laterals, farm roads, the airlines and other features of a modern transportation system have moved the smaller cities and communities of this country into the mainstream of crime and the criminal. The mobility of the criminal population and the increasing volume of local offenders have pushed the problems of crime and delinquency into a foreground position in every community, regardless of size.

Moving toward the preventive role of the police, Chapter 2 presents a review of the measures society has developed thus far over the years in the approach to this social problem, beginning with the movement toward regulation and control spearheaded by the noted Italian criminologist, Caesar Bonesana Beccaria. His work, *An Essay on Crimes and Punishments,* written in 1764 at the age of twenty-six, is conceded to be the most influential volume on the reform of criminal justice ever produced.

Thus began the era of rational enforcement in which a heavy emphasis was placed on the crime or criminal offense and the thesis of punishment as the major strategy in combatting the crime problem. Near the turn of the century, there followed a shift in interest away from the crime per se toward the criminal offender as an individual and the contributing factors that led to the end result. It is to be noted that three other Italian criminologists pioneered the way in this new approach to the problem: Caesare Lombroso (1836-1909) and his proteges, Raffaele Garofolo (1852-1934) and Enrico Ferri (1856-1929). Lombroso's concept that progress in this important area of social control pivoted on a scientific study of the individual offender was a monumental contribution.

His theory of the "atavistic throw-back" and the "criminal type" was followed in turn by the convictions of Garofolo and Ferri that the criminal offender was in large part a social product, and that in order to be understood the forces in his environment, both internal and external (biological and social) that produced him must be scientifically explored and analyzed.

During the past quarter century or more, the literature of criminology, including the prodigious works of Eleanor and Sheldon Glueck, has expanded at a rapidly increasing rate. It is concerned almost completely with a shift in emphasis toward the prevention of delinquency and crime and the rehabilitation of offenders who have already made their contact with the law, rather than with punishment as a deterrent and as a tool of reformation and control.

The futility of relying upon enforcement alone as the total answer is factored and analyzed in Chapter 3. Despite the investigative resources now at the disposal of the police, in terms of personnel, equipment and techniques, and their unparalleled performance in the application of enforcement pressure as the instrument of control, crime rates continue to mount almost ten times faster than the rate of population increase.

These discouraging facts have prompted the police to look in other directions for more effective measures of control. In casting about for solutions, recognition has long since gained foothold in police circles that the enforcement process must be re-enforced and augmented by a strong preventive effort out in the community to the end that this needless sacrifice of human life and its important values may be reduced to more acceptable dimensions.

In this direction, the records show that in the analysis of thousands of criminal careers, the young delinquent in the majority of cases is the forerunner of the adult criminal offender. But that is not enough. However disconcerting it may be, the records of the police and evidence uncovered by research reveal that an all-out attack upon the problem at the age level of juvenile delinquency holds limited promise of substantial gain in the reduction of crime.

The necessity is clearly indicated for working further upstream in the life of the youngster with problems during the formative years when behavior patterns are just beginning to take form. Studies have pointed out that delinquency and crime in the majority of cases stem from early life maladjustments and that delinquent juveniles and adult criminals displayed in almost every case the symptoms of their future misconduct as early behavior problems.

The records show that in the majority of cases, they started their abortive development in early childhood and progressed by almost imperceptible degrees into delinquent and criminal offenders. Early discovery, diagnosis and the application of adjustment measures in behalf of the physically, mentally or socially different child are gradually opening the door to promising opportunities for the prevention of delinquency and crime.

The first three chapters serve as a foundation for the police approach to delinquency and crime prevention. They draw the dimensions of delinquency and crime in the United States and offer an overview of the measures society has taken thus far toward the regulation and control of the problem. They provide an introduction to the ensuing chapters which are devoted exclusively to the police role in the total project of delinquency and crime prevention.

The strategic position of the police is emphasized in Chapter 4, together with police organization for delinquency and crime prevention. There follows an analysis of patrol beat responsibility in the total operation. The prevention unit, its functions and operational techniques are clearly defined, pointing the way for the smaller department in developing a sound and effective prevention program. Departmental policy with respect to the discovery and referral of juvenile cases and police participation in the treatment or adjustment process, are given extended treatment. The organization of community resources useful in promoting youth welfare and a review of enabling legislation at the federal level are also presented.

Collateral elements of the prevention program are set forth in Chapter 5, including the personnel factor and the juvenile records system. Carrying out a delinquency prevention program requires a superior man in police uniform, superior recruiting standards, a superior training program and a salary structure that will attract this calibre of personnel. Equally important is the care that must be exercised in the selection of juvenile officers.

The records system, mainspring of a police organization, is given appropriate attention. Accurate and complete information must be available to the chief and his personnel concerning the nature, extent and distribution of delinquency and crime in the community. Only a well-organized and well-administered police records system can satisfy this demand.

The distinction between offense records in the records division and records maintained by the prevention unit must be clearly set forth. Furthermore, the confidential nature of all police records must be respected at all times, and this is especially true of juvenile records in the prevention unit. Departmental policy with respect to the fingerprinting of juveniles is considered, including guidelines recommended by the International Association of Chiefs of Police. The necessity for a central, either county or area, juvenile index is also emphasized.

The final chapter, "Reducing the Opportunity," must be rated equally as high in importance as any other section of the book. The truth is that conditions and circumstances in the average community—most of them easily modified or eliminated altogether—are an open invitation to delinquency and crime. Here the police are presented with an unparalleled opportunity to drive downward the statistics of crime and delinquency. Chapter 6 clearly outlines the procedures that can be invoked by the police to accomplish this end.

Police Crime Prevention has been written as a manual and convenient reference work for the chief and his officers in small and medium-sized police departments. It should prove useful as a tool in local police training programs and in regional in-service training schools, as well as in courses at the university and college level. The individual police officer may find it to be a useful addition to his personal library as a source of reference and study in preparation for advancement in this professional field.

V. A. LEONARD

CONTENTS

POLICE

CRIME

PREVENTION

Our earth is degenerate in these latter days. There are signs that the world is coming to an end. The youngsters show a disrespect for their elders and a contempt for authority in every form. Crime is rampant among our young people and vandalism is general. The nation is in peril.

—Written by a discouraged Egyptian priest 3,000 years ago.

Chapter 1

THE ENIGMA OF DELINQUENCY
AND CRIME

THE EGYPTIAN priest would find little comfort upon taking a look at the massive crime rates that prevail today. Nor would he be inspired by the circumstances that in all categories of major or index crime—homicide, rape, robbery, aggravated assault, burglary, larceny and automobile theft—22 per cent of all arrests in 1969 were of persons under the age of fifteen, and almost 50 per cent were under eighteen years of age.*

Human behavior is the most overwhelming fact of life. Examined at every economic, social, political, cultural and moral level, it transcends in magnitude all other considerations. Since the dawn of recorded history, it has been and is today, humanity's chief concern all the way from the rostrum of the United Nations to the second grade classroom and the child guidance clinic. In the long struggle of mankind for self-control, human behavior has played a major role in the generation of social problems that plague an organized society. Foremost on the list of social liabilities is the problem of crime and the criminal.

Technological achievements of man during the past quarter century, including the landing of men on the moon, contemplated excursions into planetary space and the development of atomic power, stir the imagination. There is little evidence of a comparable advance in the social sciences, particularly in those

---

*Federal Bureau of Investigation, *Uniform Crime Reports*, 1969. Index crimes are those listed above. They were selected by the Bureau on the basis of importance and regularity of occurrence as an abbreviated and convenient measure of the crime problem.

areas of inquiry concerned with human behavior. The literature of the behavior sciences—including sociology, anthropology, biology, psychology, psychiatry and genetics—is voluminous, but there is much ground to be covered and much research to be undertaken before impressive guidelines are available in the approach to the problem of crime and the criminal. Yet as will be seen on the pages to come, there are bright spots on the horizon as man begins to develop measures which hold encouraging promise for the years ahead.

Meanwhile, society continues to be plagued by mounting crime rates that in recent years have increased more than ten times faster than the rate of population increase. The Uniform Crime Reporting Program, administered by the Federal Bureau of Investigation, employs seven crime classifications to establish an index to measure the trend and distribution of crime in the United States. These crimes—murder, forcible rape, robbery, aggravated assault, burglary, larceny—fifty dollars and over in value, and automobile theft—are counted by law enforcement agencies as the crimes become known to them and reported monthly to the Federal Bureau of Investigation. They were selected for use in the Crime Index because as a group they represent the most common local crime problem.

They are all serious crimes, either by their very nature or due to the volume in which they occur. Offenses of murder, forcible rape, robbery and aggravated assault are classified as violent crimes. The offenses of burglary, larceny over fifty dollars in value, and automobile theft are classed as crimes against property.

In the calendar year 1969, almost five million Index offenses were reported to law enforcement agencies. During this period, there were an estimated 14,590 murders committed in the United States, an increase of 940 over the 13,650 homicides recorded in 1968. This also represents the smallest absolute rise of murder in one year since the 600 total increase in 1965 over 1964. This crime makes up slightly more than 2 per cent of the crimes of violence and represents less than one-half of 1 per cent of all Crime Index offenses.

Uniform Crime Reports further revealed that during 1969 there was an estimated total of 306,420 aggravated assaults, an increase of 24,020 offenses over the previous year. This violent crime against the person made up over 6 per cent of the Crime Index offenses. For each 100,000 persons in the United States, there were 152 victims of aggravated assault. During 1969 there was an estimated total of 36,470 forcible rapes, an increase of 5,410 offenses over 1968. The volume of forcible rape offenses

CHART I

CRIME AND POPULATION
1960 - 1969
PERCENT CHANGE OVER 1960

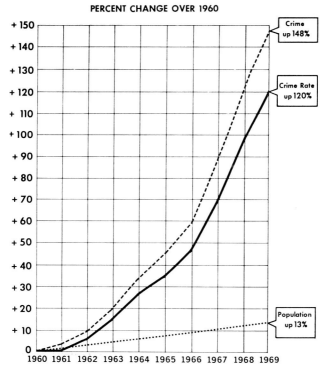

CRIME - CRIME INDEX OFFENSES
CRIME RATE - NUMBER OF OFFENSES PER 100,000 POPULATION

Reproduced through the courtesy of the Federal Bureau of Investigation.

CHART II

MURDER
1960 - 1969

PERCENT CHANGE OVER 1960
------- NUMBER OF OFFENSES UP 62 PERCENT
———— RATE PER 100,000 INHABITANTS UP 44 PERCENT

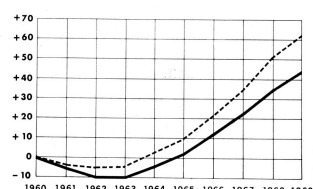

Reproduced through the courtesy of the Federal Bureau of Investigation.

CHART III

AGGRAVATED ASSAULT
1960 - 1969

PERCENT CHANGE OVER 1960
- - - NUMBER OF OFFENSES UP 102 PERCENT
———— RATE PER 100,000 INHABITANTS UP 79 PERCENT

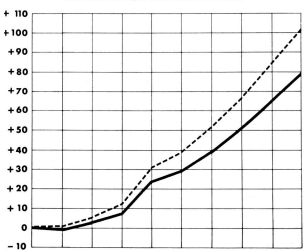

Reproduced through the courtesy of the Federal Bureau of Investigation.

in 1969 increased 17 per cent over 1968, and 116 per cent over 1960.

In 1969 robbery offenses increased 14 per cent in volume compared with 1968. Since 1960 robbery has increased 177 per cent. The robbery rate of 147 victims per 100,000 inhabitants was 13 per cent above the 1968 rate and 146 per cent above the 1960 rate. Bank robbery increased in volume by 296 per cent over 1960. An estimated total of 1,949,800 burglaries occurred during 1969. Volume-wise this was an increase of 120,900 offenses over 1968. Larceny over fifty dollars in value was the second most voluminous Index crime, exceeded only by burglary. In 1969 there were 1,512,900 cases recorded, up from 1,271,000 in 1968. This crime makes up 30 per cent of the Crime Index total.

CHART IV

FORCIBLE RAPE
1960 - 1969

PERCENT CHANGE OVER 1960

- - - - NUMBER OF OFFENSES UP 116 PERCENT
——— RATE PER 100,000 INHABITANTS UP 93 PERCENT

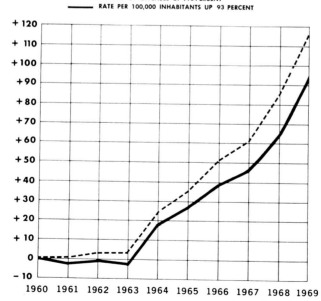

Reproduced through the courtesy of the Federal Bureau of Investigation.

Uniform Crime Reports show that during 1969, 871,900 motor vehicles were reported stolen compared to 777,800 in 1968, an increase of 12 per cent over 1968. This offense has been steadily rising each year since 1960, with an over-all increase of 168 per cent from 1960 through 1969. From 1960 through 1969, the percentage increase in automobile theft has been four times greater than the percentage increase in automobile registrations.

CHART V

ROBBERY
1960 - 1969

PERCENT CHANGE OVER 1960
- - - - NUMBER OF OFFENSES UP 177 PERCENT
———— RATE PER 100,000 INHABITANTS UP 146 PERCENT

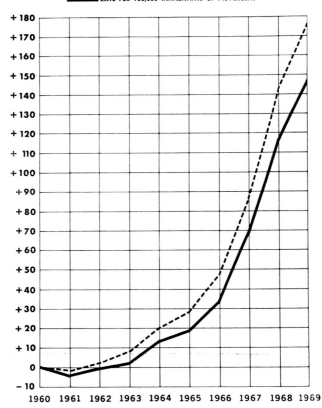

Reproduced through the courtesy of the Federal Bureau of Investigation.

The foregoing is only a part of the story. The actual situation is far more serious and far more grave than the available statistics indicate. The President's Commission on Law Enforcement and Administration of Justice found that due to the amount of unreported crime, the nation's score on the crime front was several times greater than the totals revealed in Uniform Crime Reports.°

As a part of its assignment, the Commission initiated the first national survey of crime victimization and included in its report the following information concerning the volume of crime unreported to the police.

CHART VI

BURGLARY
1960 - 1969

PERCENT CHANGE OVER 1960

- - - - NUMBER OF OFFENSES UP 117 PERCENT
——— RATE PER 100,000 INHABITANTS UP 93 PERCENT

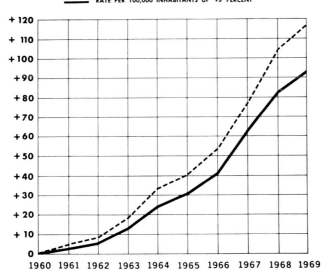

Reproduced through the courtesy of the Federal Bureau of Investigation.

°President's Commission on Law Enforcement and Administration of Justice. *The Challenge of Crime in a Free Society,* Washington, U. S. Gov. Print. Office, 1967, p. 20.

CHART VII

LARCENY
($50 AND OVER)
1960 - 1969

PERCENT CHANGE OVER 1960
- - - NUMBER OF OFFENSES UP 199 PERCENT
—— RATE PER 100,000 INHABITANTS UP 165 PERCENT

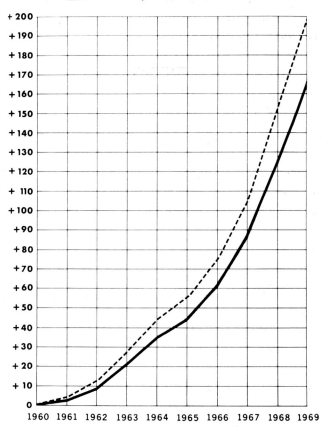

Reproduced through the courtesy of the Federal Bureau of Investigation.

CHART VIII

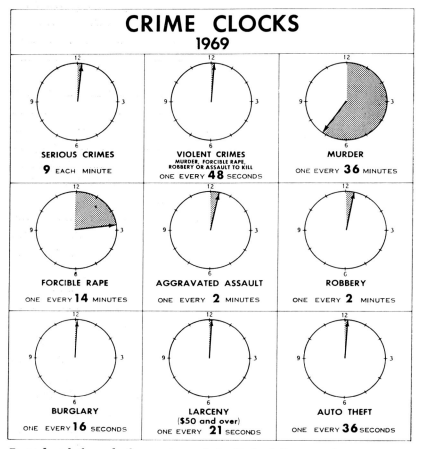

CRIME CLOCKS
1969

SERIOUS CRIMES
9 EACH MINUTE

VIOLENT CRIMES
MURDER, FORCIBLE RAPE,
ROBBERY OR ASSAULT TO KILL
ONE EVERY **48** SECONDS

MURDER
ONE EVERY **36** MINUTES

FORCIBLE RAPE
ONE EVERY **14** MINUTES

AGGRAVATED ASSAULT
ONE EVERY **2** MINUTES

ROBBERY
ONE EVERY **2** MINUTES

BURGLARY
ONE EVERY **16** SECONDS

LARCENY
($50 and over)
ONE EVERY **21** SECONDS

AUTO THEFT
ONE EVERY **36** SECONDS

Reproduced through the courtesy of the Federal Bureau of Investigation.

UNREPORTED CRIME

Although Uniform Crime Reports reveal a crime volume of disturbing proportions, they hardly begin to indicate the full amount. Crimes reported directly to prosecutors usually do not show up on the police statistics. Citizens often do not report crimes to the police. Some crimes reported to the police never get into the statistical system.

The National Opinion Research Center of the University of

Chicago, working under the auspices of the Commission, surveyed 10,000 households, asking whether the person questioned, or any member of his or her household, had been a victim of crime during the past year. Inquiry was also made as to whether the crime had been reported and, if not, the reason for not reporting.

More detailed surveys were undertaken in a number of high and medium crime rate precincts of Washington, Chicago and Boston by the Bureau of Social Science Research of Washington, D. C., and by the Survey Research Center of the University of Michigan. All of the surveys dealt primarily with households or individuals, although some data were obtained for certain kinds of businesses and other organizations.

These surveys show that the actual amount of crime in the United States is several times the amount reported in Uniform Crime Reports. The data indicated that the number of forcible rapes was more than three and a half times the reported rate; burglaries, three times; aggravated assault and larcenies over fifty dollars in value, more than double. The incidence of robbery was 50 per cent greater than the reported rate.

Even these rates probably understate the actual amount of crime committed in this country. The Washington, Boston and Chicago surveys, based solely upon victimization of the person interviewed, show even more clearly the disparity between reported and unreported crime. The clearest case is that of the survey in three Washington precincts, where, for the purpose of comparing survey results with crimes reported to the police, previous special studies made it possible to eliminate from police statistics crimes involving business and transient victims. In connection with certain specific offenses against individuals, the number of offenses reported to the survey per thousand residents (18 years or over) ranged, depending on the offense, from three to ten times greater than the number contained in police statistics.

The survey in Boston and in one of the Chicago precincts indicated about three times as many Index crimes as police statistics showed; in the other Chicago precinct, about one and a half times as many were indicated.

Thus, crimes reported to the police represent only a fraction of the number that actually occur. Shulman observed that, in the face of social resistance against reporting and the opportunities for concealment, unreported criminal offenses probably number in the millions of cases and far exceed in both volume and monetary loss the number of offenses that are reported to the police.*

In terms of criminal offenses reported to the police, the first nine months of 1970 offered little encouragement, with the spiral upward still in evidence. During this period, crime in the United States, as measured by the Crime Index, increased 10 per cent when compared with the same period in 1969. The violent crimes as a group were up 10 per cent. Robbery increased 15 per cent, murder 9 per cent, aggravated assault 7 per cent, and forcible rape 2 per cent. Larceny fifty dollars and over in value was up 14 per cent, burglary 9 per cent, and automobile theft 6 per cent. Cities having a population of 250,000 or more experienced an average increase of 6 per cent; *suburban law enforcement agencies reported a 14 per cent rise, and the rural areas were up 9 per cent.*

It will be noted in the tables that follow that the nation's score on the crime front for 1970 was again dominated by plus signs.

> During calendar year 1970 crime in the United States, as measured by the Crime Index offenses, increased 11 per cent over 1969. The violent crimes as a group rose 12 per cent with robbery up 17 per cent, murder and aggravated assault up 7 per cent and forcible rape up 2 per cent. The property crimes increased 10 per cent. Larceny fifty dollars and over was up 14 per cent, burglary 10 per cent and auto theft 5 per cent. Crime in the large core cities with 250,000 or more inhabitants increased 6 per cent, suburban areas reported a 15 per cent rise and the rural areas 14 per cent (Table I). Geographically, the Southern States reported an increase

*Shulman, Harry Manuel, The measurement of crime in the United States, *J. Crim. L.C. & P.S.*, 57 (No. 4), December, 1966.

TABLE I

CRIME INDEX TRENDS

(Per cent change 1970 over 1969, offenses known to the police)

Population Group and Area	Number of Agencies	Population in Thousands	Total	Violent	Property	Murder	Forcible Rape	Robbery	Aggravated Assault	Burglary	Larceny, $50 and Over	Auto Theft
Total all agencies	5,244	157,942	+11	+12	+10	+7	+2	+17	+7	+10	+14	+5
Cities over 25,000	835	90,086	+9	+12	+9	+7	+3	+17	+6	+10	+11	+5
Suburban area	2,031	47,078	+15	+13	+15	+5	—	+21	+10	+13	+20	+10
Rural area	1,146	18,209	+14	+7	+15	+11	+5	+14	+6	+11	+24	+3
Over 1,000,000	6	19,537	+8	+13	+6	+11	−2	+21	+1	+7	+2	+9
500,000 to 1,000,000	20	13,055	+3	+6	+2	+3	+1	+8	+4	+5	+6	−4
250,000 to 500,000	30	10,652	+8	+12	+8	+8	+5	+14	+10	+11	+8	+3
100,000 to 250,000	93	13,788	+14	+12	+14	+13	+10	+17	+8	+15	+16	+7
50,000 to 100,000	251	17,468	+14	+14	+14	+2	+10	+18	+12	+13	+18	+7
25,000 to 50,000	435	15,586	+15	+17	+15	+3	+2	+25	+14	+14	+18	+8
10,000 to 25,000	1,118	17,776	+15	+15	+15	−10	−2	+19	+16	+12	+21	+10
Under 10,000	1,873	9,779	+14	+11	+15	−6	+11	+16	+11	+10	+21	+9

The Enigma of Delinquency and Crime

TABLE II

CRIME INDEX TRENDS BY GEOGRAPHIC REGION

(1970 over 1969)

Region	Total	Violent	Property	Murder	Forcible Rape	Robbery	Aggravated Assault	Burglary	Larceny, $50 and Over	Auto Theft
Northeastern States	+10	+17	+9	+13	+1	+24	+8	+8	+11	+9
North Central States	+11	+10	+11	+8	+1	+16	+4	+12	+16	+1
Southern States	+13	+11	+13	+4	+4	+15	+9	+12	+18	+6
Western States	+9	+5	+9	+6	+1	+6	+5	+10	+11	+4

TABLE III

CRIME INDEX TRENDS

(Per cent change 1965-1970, each year over previous year)

Years	Total	Violent	Property	Murder	Forcible Rape	Robbery	Aggravated Assault	Burglary	Larceny, $50 and Over	Auto Theft
1966/1965	+11	+11	+11	+11	+10	+14	+9	+10	+13	+13
1967/1966	+16	+16	+17	+11	+7	+28	+9	+16	+17	+18
1968/1967	+17	+19	+17	+13	+15	+30	+11	+14	+21	+19
1969/1968	+12	+11	+12	+7	+17	+14	+9	+7	+19	+12
1970/1969	+11	+12	+10	+7	+2	+17	+7	+10	+14	+5

of 13 per cent in the Crime Index offenses, the North Central States 11 per cent, the Northeastern States 10 per cent and the Western States 9 per cent (Table II). Armed robbery, which makes up about two-thirds of all robbery offenses, recorded an increase of 20 per cent during the year. Aggravated assaults committed with firearms increased 10 per cent.[*]

THE COST OF CRIME

One way in which crime affects the lives of all Americans is that it costs all Americans money. Crime in the United States today imposes a very heavy economic burden upon the community as a whole and upon every individual member of the community. Chart IV indicates that crime and the criminal is costing the people of this country more than 20 billion dollars annually. The costs of lost or damaged lives, of fear and suffering cannot be measured solely in dollars and cents. As early as 1941, Carr[†] observed, "In some parts of the nation it is actually a question whether thugs or decent people are sovereign in the community. Certainly a forced 'tax' by crookdom each year of more than orderly government can raise for education makes one wonder what sovereignty amounts to if it cannot protect its own people against such tribute."

The notion that crime was primarily a problem of the larger cities has long since been abandoned. Freeways, major arterials, laterals, farm roads and other features of a modern highway system have moved the smaller cities and communities into the mainstream of the nation's theatre of crime and the criminal. Mobility of the criminal population, along with an increasing volume of local offenders, have pushed the problems of crime and delinquency into a foreground position in every community, regardless of size. The following tables reveal the arrest record in suburban and rural areas for 1969.[‡] Tables I and II are of

---

[*]Issued by John Edgar Hoover, Director, Federal Bureau of Investigation, United States Department of Justice, Washington, D. C. 20535. (Includes Tables I, II, and III following.)

[†]Carr, L. J., *Delinquency Control*, New York, Harper & Bros., 1941, p. 35.

[‡]Federal Bureau of Investigation, *Uniform Crime Reports*, Washington, U. S. Gov. Print. Office, 1969.

special interest since they provide information concerning arrests by age groups from under fifteen to under twenty-one.

CHART IX

Economic Impact of Crimes and Related Expenditures
(Estimated in Millions of Dollars)

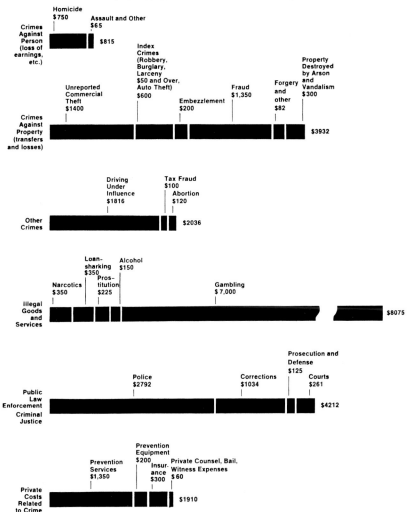

President's Commission on Law Enforcement and Administration of Justice, *Task Force Report: Crime and Its Impact—An Assessment,* Washington, U. S. Gov. Print. Office, p. 44.

TABLE IV

SUBURBAN ARREST TRENDS, 1968-1969

[1,553 agencies, 1969 estimated population 35,563,000]

Offense Charged	Total All Ages			Number of Persons Arrested Under 18 Years of Age			18 Years of Age and Over		
	1968	1969	Per Cent Change	1968	1969	Per Cent Change	1968	1969	Per Cent Change
Total	903,804	977,254	+ 8.1	324,068	342,949	+ 5.8	579,736	634,305	+ 9.4
Criminal homicide:									
(a) Murder and non-negligent manslaughter	1,201	1,233	+ 2.7	133	81	− 39.1	1,068	1,152	+ 7.9
(b) Manslaughter by negligence	576	580	+ .7	43	51	+18.6	533	529	− .8
Forcible rape	2,251	2,366	+ 5.1	420	425	+ 1.2	1,831	1,941	+ 6.0
Robbery	7,588	8,123	+ 7.1	2,039	2,193	+ 7.6	5,549	5,930	+ 6.9
Aggravated assault	16,048	17,681	+10.2	2,640	3,012	+14.1	13,408	14,669	+ 9.4
Burglary—breaking or entering	51,579	52,246	+ 1.3	30,259	30,359	+ .3	21,320	21,887	+ 2.7
Larceny—theft	92,805	102,371	+10.3	54,237	57,715	+ 6.4	38,568	44,656	+15.8
Auto theft	21,906	21,640	− 1.2	13,985	13,222	− 5.5	7,921	8,418	+ 6.3
Violent crime	27,088	29,403	+ 8.5	5,232	5,711	+ 9.2	21,856	23,692	+ 8.4
Property crime	166,290	176,257	+ 6.0	98,481	101,296	+ 2.9	67,809	74,961	+10.5
Subtotal for above offenses	193,954	206,240	+ 6.3	103,756	107,058	+ 3.2	90,198	99,182	+10.0

Offense									
Other assaults	42,748	45,493	+6.4	8,049	8,348	+3.7	34,699	37,145	+7.0
Arson	1,976	1,960	−.8	1,446	1,414	−2.2	530	546	+3.0
Forgery and counterfeiting	6,442	6,181	−4.1	737	758	+2.8	5,705	5,423	−4.9
Fraud	12,306	13,288	+8.0	362	448	+23.8	11,944	12,840	+7.5
Embezzlement	1,606	1,588	−1.1	44	40	−9.1	1,562	1,548	−.9
Stolen property; buying, receiving and possessing	6,450	8,124	+26.0	2,502	2,977	+19.0	3,948	5,147	+30.4
Vandalism	26,798	25,987	−3.0	22,630	21,683	−4.2	4,168	4,304	+3.3
Weapons; carrying, possessing, etc.	10,668	11,070	+3.8	3,040	2,849	−6.3	7,628	8,221	+7.8
Prostitution and commercialized vice	1,469	1,934	+31.7	22	28	+27.3	1,447	1,906	+31.7
Sex offenses (except forcible rape and prostitution)	8,433	8,753	+3.8	2,450	2,343	−4.4	5,983	6,410	+7.1
Narcotic drug laws	34,223	47,228	+38.0	12,044	14,396	+19.5	22,179	32,832	+48.0
Gambling	3,999	3,785	−5.4	200	137	−31.5	3,799	3,648	−4.0
Offenses against family and children	11,312	11,438	+1.1	202	288	+42.6	11,110	11,150	+.4
Driving under the influence	61,581	72,380	+17.5	757	1,003	+32.5	60,824	71,377	+17.4
Liquor laws	44,164	48,634	+10.1	18,059	20,450	+13.2	26,105	28,184	+8.0
Drunkenness	142,364	149,991	+5.4	9,692	12,118	+25.0	132,672	137,873	+3.9
Disorderly conduct	88,880	90,796	+2.2	26,633	27,641	+3.8	62,247	63,155	+1.5
Vagrancy	9,303	7,782	−16.3	1,469	1,239	−15.7	7,834	6,543	−16.5
All other offenses (except traffic)	132,967	147,494	+10.9	47,813	50,623	+5.9	85,154	96,871	+13.8
Suspicion (not included in totals)	10,419	12,415	+19.2	3,619	5,145	+42.2	6,800	7,270	+6.9
Curfew and loitering law violations	22,891	23,673	+3.4	22,891	23,673	+3.4	......	......	......
Runaways	39,270	43,435	+10.6	39,270	43,435	+10.6	......	......	......

Violent crime is offenses of murder, forcible rape, robbery and aggravated assault.

Property crime is offenses of burglary, larceny $50 and over and auto theft.

TABLE V

SUBURBAN ARRESTS OF PERSONS UNDER 15, UNDER 18, UNDER 21, AND UNDER 25 YEARS OF AGE, 1969

[1,790 agencies; 1969 estimated population 39,895,000]

Offense Charged	Total	Number of Persons Arrested				Percentage			
		Under 15	Under 18	Under 21	Under 25	Under 15	Under 18	Under 21	Under 25
Total	1,120,002	144,683	389,232	565,384	702,408	12.9	34.8	50.5	62.7
Criminal homicide:									
(a) Murder and non-negligent manslaughter	1,487	11	96	314	580	.7	6.5	21.1	39.0
(b) Manslaughter by negligence	659	7	54	180	303	1.1	8.2	27.3	46.0
Forcible rape	2,764	63	474	1,141	1,841	2.3	17.1	41.3	66.6
Robbery	9,267	736	2,428	4,958	7,120	7.9	26.2	53.5	76.8
Aggravated assault	20,701	1,006	3,425	6,737	10,276	4.9	16.5	32.5	49.6
Burglary—breaking or entering	58,848	15,219	33,497	44,191	50,862	25.9	56.9	75.1	86.4
Larceny—theft	114,548	32,769	64,128	80,993	91,471	28.6	56.0	70.7	79.9
Auto theft	24,314	3,779	14,699	19,440	21,813	15.5	60.5	80.0	89.7
Violent crime	34,219	1,816	6,423	13,150	19,817	5.3	18.8	38.4	57.9
Property crime	197,710	51,767	112,324	144,624	164,146	26.2	56.8	73.1	83.0
Subtotal for above offenses	232,588	53,590	118,801	157,954	184,266	23.0	51.1	67.9	79.2

Other assaults	52,315	3,703	9,507	15,858	23,853	7.1	18.2	30.3	45.6
Arson	2,207	1,135	1,586	1,804	1,939	51.4	71.9	81.7	87.9
Forgery and counterfeiting	7,417	155	846	2,153	3,931	2.1	11.4	29.0	53.0
Fraud	16,062	108	495	1,887	5,067	.7	3.1	11.7	31.5
Embezzlement	1,732	3	44	248	634	.2	2.5	14.3	36.6
Stolen property; buying, receiving and possessing	9,124	1,063	3,309	5,338	6,823	11.7	36.3	58.5	74.8
Vandalism	30,428	16,478	25,265	27,525	28,625	54.2	83.0	90.5	94.1
Weapons; carrying, possessing, etc.	12,819	1,024	3,232	5,508	7,720	8.0	25.2	43.0	60.2
Prostitution and commercialized vice	2,008	2	34	219	1,097	.1	1.7	10.9	54.6
Sex offenses (except forcible rape and prostitution)	9,610	954	2,545	3,834	5,546	9.9	26.5	39.9	57.7
Narcotic drug laws	51,611	2,322	15,756	33,338	44,160	4.5	30.5	64.6	85.6
Gambling	4,216	36	162	344	713	.9	3.8	8.2	16.9
Offenses against family and children	13,472	84	326	1,550	3,869	.6	2.4	11.5	28.7
Driving under the influence	80,575	8	1,116	6,439	17,042	°	1.4	8.0	21.2
Liquor laws	55,381	2,082	23,227	47,214	50,366	3.8	41.9	85.3	90.9
Drunkenness	168,742	1,819	13,357	30,972	51,307	1.1	7.9	18.4	30.4
Disorderly conduct	102,879	11,604	31,263	50,524	66,159	11.3	30.4	49.1	64.3
Vagrancy	9,222	245	1,318	3,587	5,009	2.7	14.3	38.9	54.3
All other offenses (except traffic)	168,837	22,334	56,723	85,286	108,423	13.2	33.6	50.5	64.2
Suspicion (not included in totals)	13,962	1,666	5,525	9,007	11,064	11.9	39.6	64.5	79.2
Curfew and loitering law violations	26,606	5,871	26,606	26,606	26,606	22.1	100.0	100.0	100.0
Runaways	48,189	18,397	48,189	48,189	48,189	38.2	100.0	100.0	100.0

*Less than one-tenth of 1 per cent.
Violent crime is offenses of murder, forcible rape, robbery and aggravated assault.
Property crime is offenses of burglary, larceny $50 and over and auto theft.

TABLE VI

RURAL ARREST TRENDS, 1968-69

[800 agencies; 1969 estimated population 13,853,000]

Offense Charged	Number of Persons Arrested								
	Total All Ages			Under 18 Years of Age			18 Years of Age and Over		
	1968	1969	Per Cent Change	1968	1969	Per Cent Change	1968	1969	Per Cent Change
Total	234,665	244,061	+ 4.0	50,285	51,732	+ 2.9	184,380	192,329	+ 4.3
Criminal homicide:									
(a) Murder and non-negligent manslaughter	560	536	− 4.3	37	19	− 48.6	523	517	− 1.1
(b) Manslaughter by negligence	414	429	+ 3.6	28	14	− 50.0	386	415	+ 7.5
Forcible rape	858	847	− 1.3	123	101	− 17.9	735	746	+ 1.5
Robbery	1,203	1,416	+17.7	157	194	+23.6	1,046	1,222	+16.8
Aggravated assault	4,798	4,676	− 2.5	332	343	+ 3.3	4,466	4,333	− 3.0
Burglary—breaking or entering	14,513	15,572	+ 7.3	6,643	7,263	+ 9.3	7,870	8,309	+ 5.6
Larceny—theft	14,564	15,221	+ 4.5	5,423	5,319	− 1.9	9,141	9,902	+ 8.3
Auto theft	4,570	4,320	− 5.5	2,387	2,270	− 4.9	2,183	2,050	− 6.1
Violent crime	7,419	7,475	+ .8	649	657	+ 1.2	6,770	6,818	+ .7
Property crime	33,647	35,113	+ 4.4	14,453	14,852	+ 2.8	19,194	20,261	+ 5.6
Subtotal for above offenses	41,480	43,017	+ 3.7	15,130	15,523	+ 2.6	26,350	27,494	+ 4.3

Other assaults	8,685	8,949	+3.0	672	619	−7.9	8,013	8,330	+4.0
Arson	623	566	−9.1	278	210	−24.5	345	356	+3.2
Forgery and counterfeiting	2,541	2,427	−4.5	241	269	+11.6	2,300	2,158	−6.2
Fraud	6,295	7,135	+13.3	88	95	+8.0	6,207	7,040	+13.4
Embezzlement	279	315	+12.9	10	6	−40.0	269	309	+14.9
Stolen property; buying, receiving and possessing	1,959	2,167	+10.6	450	572	+27.1	1,509	1,595	+5.7
Vandalism	5,596	4,953	−11.5	3,522	3,077	−12.6	2,074	1,876	−9.5
Weapons; carrying, possessing, etc.	2,646	2,625	−.8	307	263	−14.3	2,339	2,362	+1.0
Prostitution and commercialized vice	256	301	+17.6	11	14	+27.3	245	287	+17.1
Sex offenses (except forcible rape and prostitution)	1,806	1,878	+4.0	347	325	−6.3	1,459	1,553	+6.4
Narcotic drug laws	3,151	5,823	+84.8	637	1,044	+63.9	2,514	4,779	+90.1
Gambling	1,747	2,375	+35.9	39	16	−59.0	1,708	2,359	+38.1
Offenses against family and children	6,551	6,439	−1.7	57	85	+49.1	6,494	6,354	−2.2
Driving under the influence	21,997	25,275	+14.9	199	398	+100.0	21,798	24,877	+14.1
Liquor laws	21,967	21,828	−.6	7,210	7,178	−.4	14,757	14,650	−.7
Drunkenness	39,982	39,168	−2.0	1,553	1,709	+10.0	38,429	37,459	−2.5
Disorderly conduct	13,552	12,862	−5.1	1,888	1,733	−8.2	11,664	11,129	−4.6
Vagrancy	2,712	2,114	−22.1	227	196	−13.7	2,485	1,918	−22.8
All other offenses (except traffic)	41,503	44,533	+7.3	8,082	9,089	+12.5	33,421	35,444	+6.1
Suspicion (not included in totals)	1,153	1,215	+5.4	438	552	+26.0	715	663	−7.3
Curfew and loitering law violations	1,673	1,554	−7.1	1,673	1,554	−7.1	......	......	......
Runaways	7,664	7,757	+1.2	7,664	7,757	+1.2	......	......	......

Violent crime is offenses of murder, forcible rape, robbery and aggravated assault.

Property crime is offenses of burglary, larceny $50 and over and auto theft.

TABLE VII

RURAL ARRESTS OF PERSONS UNDER 15, UNDER 18, UNDER 21, AND UNDER 25 YEARS OF AGE, 1969

[1,094 agencies; 1969 estimated population 17,578,000]

Offense Charged	Grand Total All Ages	Number of Persons Arrested				Percentage			
		Under 15	Under 18	Under 21	Under 25	Under 15	Under 18	Under 21	Under 25
Total	309,693	15,386	64,588	119,043	162,860	5.0	20.9	38.4	52.6
Criminal homicide:									
(a) Murder and non-negligent manslaughter	837	6	32	138	295	.7	3.8	16.5	35.2
(b) Manslaughter by negligence	659	1	27	140	297	.2	4.1	21.2	45.1
Forcible rape	1,098	16	139	426	719	1.5	12.7	38.8	65.5
Robbery	1,867	31	260	744	1,241	1.7	13.9	39.9	66.5
Aggravated assault	6,147	57	440	1,357	2,549	.9	7.2	22.1	41.5
Burglary—breaking or entering	19,362	2,796	8,736	13,479	16,235	14.4	45.1	69.9	83.8
Larceny—theft	19,122	1,863	6,465	11,356	14,158	9.7	33.8	59.4	74.0
Auto theft	6,720	692	3,275	4,716	5,591	10.3	48.7	70.2	83.2
Violent crime	9,949	110	871	2,665	4,804	1.1	8.8	26.8	48.3
Property crime	45,204	5,351	18,476	29,551	35,984	11.8	40.9	65.4	79.6
Subtotal for above offenses	55,812	5,462	19,374	32,356	41,085	9.8	34.7	58.0	73.6

Other assaults	11,278	147	762	2,165	4,185	1.3	6.8	19.2	37.1
Arson	757	125	265	420	521	16.5	35.0	55.5	68.8
Forgery and counterfeiting	2,971	37	311	846	1,457	1.2	10.5	28.5	49.0
Fraud	8,500	12	131	880	2,493	.1	1.5	10.4	29.3
Embezzlement	464	2	14	48	142	.4	3.0	10.3	30.6
Stolen property; buying, receiving and possessing	2,701	131	701	1,403	1,878	4.9	26.0	51.9	69.5
Vandalism	5,710	1,624	3,503	4,653	5,147	28.4	61.3	81.5	90.1
Weapons; carrying, possessing, etc.	3,404	74	308	825	1,547	2.2	9.0	24.2	45.4
Prostitution and commercialized vice	352	1	14	60	164	.3	4.0	17.0	46.6
Sex offenses (except forcible rape and prostitution)	2,391	114	401	799	1,236	4.8	16.8	33.4	51.7
Narcotic drug laws	7,084	109	1,309	4,126	6,014	1.5	18.5	58.2	84.9
Gambling	2,534	7	22	72	194	.3	.9	2.8	7.7
Offenses against family and children	7,537	28	113	715	2,024	.4	1.5	9.5	26.9
Driving under the influence	32,777	12	498	2,501	6,496	*	1.5	7.6	19.8
Liquor laws	25,514	508	8,223	19,811	21,705	2.0	32.2	77.6	85.1
Drunkenness	48,458	159	2,073	5,646	11,083	.3	4.3	11.7	22.9
Disorderly conduct	16,943	486	2,220	5,421	8,585	2.9	13.1	32.0	50.7
Vagrancy	2,581	26	236	782	1,187	1.0	9.1	30.3	46.0
All other offenses (except traffic)	58,507	3,125	11,695	22,725	32,716	5.3	20.0	38.8	55.9
Suspicion (not included in totals)	1,623	177	620	994	1,206	10.9	38.2	61.2	74.3
Curfew and loitering law violations	1,967	390	1,967	1,967	1,967	19.8	100.0	100.0	100.0
Runaways	9,828	2,630	9,828	9,828	9,828	26.8	100.0	100.0	100.0

*Less than one-tenth of 1 per cent.

Violent crime is offenses of murder, forcible rape, robbery and aggravated assault.

Property crime is offenses of burglary, larceny $50 and over and auto theft.

Chapter 1 has presented what might be termed the unglorious picture! Is it all necessary? It was and is rational for man to conclude that there must be some way to prevent or reduce the volume of crime and delinquency and give society some relief from this staggering social burden. The history of criminology, the scientific study of crime as a social phenomenon, is largely an account of the prodigious effort that has been expended in an attempt to find some of the answers.

It appears relevant at this point to consider some of the measures society has taken over the years in the approach to this major social problem—crime and the criminal.

Chapter 2

TOWARD REGULATION AND CONTROL

ASIDE from the Christian concept and doctrine, which was probably the greatest social force ever to come the way of humanity, it is well to keep in mind that two major divisions of thought have in turn presided over all attempts to control or influence human behavior in the realm of delinquency and crime.

The first directed its attention to the crime or criminal offense —essentially for our purposes here, a violation of the accepted mores or binding customs and practices of a group or community. Thus, the rule of *law* emerged—a code of conduct imposing an obligation toward obedience and enforced by a controlling authority, together with prescribed penalties or punishment for the violation of any provision of the code.

The second became concerned with the offender as an individual rather than with the crime itself—and the forces both internal and external that contributed to the end result. There followed in logical succession the philosophy of rehabilitation and that of prevention.

Until about 1800, the crime or criminal offense itself was man's primary concern. In terms of the rule of law, the Babylonian king Hammurabi, who lived about 2300 B.C., was among the first to codify existing customs and practices into a body of written law, succeeded by other codes that were promulgated from time to time. The Romans under Emperor Justinian codified a remarkable system of jurisprudence which has since influenced the character of the legal system in every nation of western Europe with the exception of England. Among his most important achievements Napoleon, in the early 1800's, aided by a committee of learned jurists, reshaped and codified the confused laws of France and gave the country a unified, rational system of law—the celebrated Code of Napoleon.

It is helpful at this point to draw the distinction between civil and criminal law, a difference that is based upon their objectives. In civil law, the objective is the redress of wrongs through compulsory restitution or compensation. Criminal law, on the other hand, seeks to punish the wrongdoer. In civil litigation, private wrongs are adjusted by lawsuits between the parties involved. In a criminal prosecution, government itself is a party, moving in where the interests of the public are at issue.*

Crimes are classified as treasons, felonies and misdemeanors. Treason is regarded as the most serious of all crimes since it involves a direct attack upon government and poses a threat to the foundations of society itself. A felony is generally construed to be a criminal offense punishable by confinement in a state or federal prison. All other crimes are classified as misdemeanors.

Conscience is not strong enough to produce unvarying conformity and compliance with accepted standards, hence, the need for some form of compulsion, which seeks expression on three fronts: religion, public opinion, and law. Of these three, we are concerned here primarily with the law and the administration of justice by the state, acting through the application of physical force.

It is one of the primary functions of organized society to protect itself from the criminal element. In the approach to this objective, the assumption is that crime control is a question of law, although it will ultimately pivot to a considerable degree on some form or forms of social prophylaxis, as in preventive medicine. This is the central thesis of the present volume.

Criminal law is the instrument of criminal policy wherein the rules are prescribed for determining whether a crime has in fact been committed; whether the accused person has com-

---

*Leonard, V. A., *The Police, the Judiciary, and the Criminal*, Springfield, Thomas, 1969, p. 5.

mitted that crime; and finally, what the sanction, penalty or punishment shall be if the subject is found guilty.

The criminal law is an important form of social control. Through it, organized society defines certain acts of human conduct as criminal and attempts to restrain these acts through a system of procedures and penalties. It operates by the imposition of sanctions, ranging from a fine or jail sentence to capital punishment, on those persons found guilty of committing crimes. Execution is the ultimate in the application of force by the state as a form of social control.

In the United States, the criminal law usually finds expression in the penal codes of the several states and in the federal codes, where criminal offenses are classified and defined, and specific penalties are prescribed for each classification. The determination of the nature and extent of criminal liability in any given instance is altogether a different matter. In actual practice, the approach to this problem is largely through the application of *stare decisis* or prior case decisions to the facts presented in the individual case. Prior legal precedents may be cited during the original trial of the case in criminal court, or on appeal before appellate courts up to, and including, the United States Supreme Court.

Hence, the criminal law in operation is to a considerable extent the operation of case-decision law flowing from interpretations handed down by the courts in a given set of case circumstances. In fact, a formal course in criminal law at any accredited law school is largely a study of case decisions.*

The companion course in the law of evidence which implements the criminal law is likewise dominated by a study of case decisions. Together, the criminal law and the law of evidence offer to the police a working blueprint for the important function of criminal investigation, the marshaling of evidence, and the presentation of the case in court by the prosecution.

---

*See Perkins, Rollin N., *Criminal Law and Procedure*, 2nd ed. Brooklyn, Foundation Press, 1959; also McCormick, Charles T., *Cases and Materials on the Law of Evidence*, 2nd ed. St. Paul, West, 1948.

CHART X

A general view of The Criminal Justice System

This chart seeks to present a simple yet comprehensive view
of the movement of cases through the criminal justice system.
Procedures in individual jurisdictions may vary from the pattern
shown here. The differing weights of line indicate the relative
volumes of cases disposed of at various points in the system,
but this is only suggestive since no nationwide data of this
sort exists.

Police   Prosecution   Courts

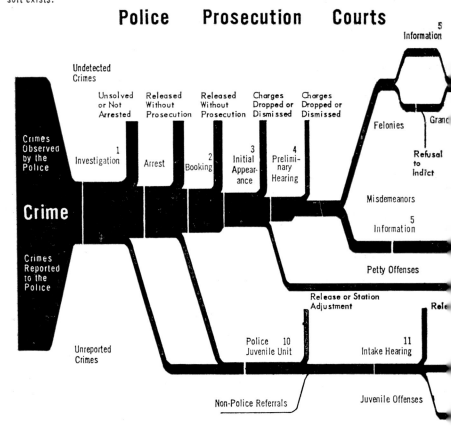

1 May continue until trial.

2 Administrative record of arrest. First
   step at which temporary release on
   bail may be available.

3 Before magistrate, commissioner, or
   justice of peace. Formal notice of
   charge, advice of rights. Bail set.
   Summary trials for petty offenses
   usually conducted here without
   further processing.

4 Preliminary testing of evidence
   against defendant. Charge may be
   reduced. No separate preliminary
   hearing for misdemeanors in some
   systems.

5 Charge filed by prosecutor on basis
   of information submitted by police
   citizens. Alternative to grand jury
   indictment; often used in felonies,
   almost always in misdemeanors.

6 Reviews whether Government
   evidence sufficient to justify trial.
   Some States have no grand jury
   system; others seldom use it.

Corrections

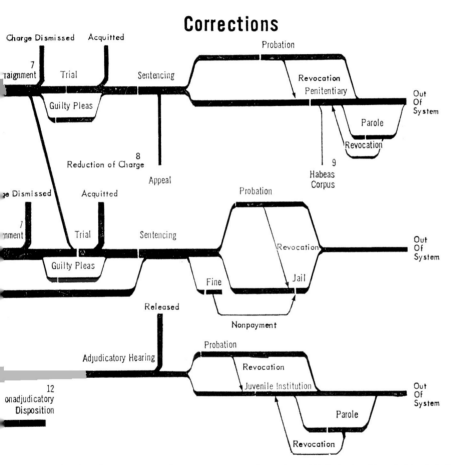

Charge Dismissed   Acquitted

Probation

7
raignment   Trial   Sentencing   Revocation

Penitentiary   Out
Of
Guilty Pleas   System

Parole

Revocation

8
Reduction of Charge   9

Appeal   Habeas
Corpus

ge Dismissed   Acquitted   Probation

7
nment   Trial   Sentencing   Revocation   Out
Of
Guilty Pleas   System

Fine   Jail

Released

Nonpayment

Probation

Adjudicatory Hearing   Revocation

Juvenile Institution   Out
Of
12   System
onadjudicatory
Disposition   Parole

Revocation

ppearance for plea; defendant
ects trial by judge or jury (if
ailable); counsel for indigent
ually appointed here in felonies.
ften not at all in other cases.

harge may be reduced at any
ne prior to trial in return for plea
guilty or for other reasons.

9 Challenge on constitutional grounds
to legality of detention. May be
sought at any point in process.

10 Police often hold informal hearings,
dismiss or adjust many cases without
further processing.

11 Probation officer decides desirability
of further court action.

12 Welfare agency, social services,
counselling, medical care, etc.,
for cases where adjudicatory
handling not needed.

* Reprinted from The President's Commission on Law Enforcement and the Administration of Justice: THE
CHALLENGE OF CRIME IN A FREE SOCIETY. Washington, D.C., Government Printing Office. February,
1967, pp. 8–9, (Catalog No. Pr 36.8: L41/C86).

It is to be noted that the criminal law is exactly what the term implies—a classification and definition of the various criminal offenses and a prescribed punishment for the commission of any of the offenses enumerated in the code. It is dedicated unmistakably to the thesis of punishment as an instrument for the prevention and control of crime and the criminal. After defining the crime of burglary, for example, the law states, "Whoever commits the crime of burglary, *shall be punished by . . .*"

A milestone in the history of the criminal law occurred in 1764 with the publication of *An Essay on Crimes and Punishments,* by Caesar Bonesana Beccaria (1738-1794),* Italian criminologist and economist. It is conceded to be the most influential volume on the reform of criminal justice ever produced.† All the more remarkable is the circumstance that it was published when the author was only twenty-six years of age.

In this book, Beccaria launched a rational and systematic attack on the savage criminal procedures and penalties of his day. He denounced the use of torture and secret proceedings in the criminal process. He was the first modern writer to subject the death penalty to fundamental criticism.

As his central thesis, Beccaria argued for the proportioning of penalties to offenses and urged that certainty of penalties is more effective than severity. He further asserted that the prevention of crime is more important than punishment. The significance of his work was immediately recognized and his book was translated into twenty-two languages. It stimulated widescale programs of reform in criminal procedure and many of the proposals Beccaria advanced have since been adopted throughout the world.

It will be recalled that the foregoing developments were concerned directly with the crime or criminal offense itself and the sanction or penalty to be assessed. It was in the early 1800's

---

*Beccaria, Caesar Bonesana, *An Essay on Crimes and Punishments,* English translation by Edward D. Ingraham, 2nd ed. Philadelphia, Philip H. Nicklin, 1819.

†*Encyclopaedia Brittanica,* vol. 3, p. 351.

that attention first began to be directed toward the offender and the factors within the individual and his environment which contributed to the criminal behavior pattern. Significantly enough, it was three other criminologists who pioneered the concept that the problem called for a scientific understanding and treatment of the offender rather than a discussion of penalties.

Cesare Lombroso (1836-1909) led the way with the thesis that the criminal was a physical type and that he could be identified by certain definite physical characteristics which were largely inherited. Lombroso spent many years of his life in European penitentiaries studying the physical characteristics of convicted criminals in an attempt to prove his thesis. His theory of the "atavistic throwback" and the "criminal type" has long since been discarded; in fact, he partially retracted it before his death in 1909.

During the summer months of 1947, the opportunity was presented the author of visiting the home and laboratory of Lombroso in Turin, Italy, as the guest of his daughter, Mrs. Enrico Carrara. In his study, library and laboratory could be seen the evidence, not only of his tireless labors in support of the original hypothesis, but of its later retraction. Noticeable on the shelves of his library was a three-volume publication entitled, "The Patient and the Weather," a treatise in the field of medicine. Lombroso had evidently recognized its implication in terms of the impact of environmental pressures upon the behavior pattern.

Appropriately enough for a criminal anthropologist, Lombroso's skeleton now stands in a glass case near the entrance to the laboratory at the University of Turin where he once worked. Inside his laboratory were a number of shelves around the walls. On each shelf were transparent glass receptacles filled with formaldehyde, each containing a human face. Lombroso had made arrangements with penitentiary authorities to saw off the face of executed criminals where the bodies were not claimed, so that he could bring these gruesome research materials back to his laboratory for further study.

Although much of his labor was expended in the attempt to

prove a false thesis, Lombroso pioneered the scientific study of the individual offender and thus opened the door to a rational study of crime causation. His concept that progress in this important area of social inquiry pivoted on a scientific study of the individual offender was a monumental contribution. Raffaele Garofolo (1852-1934) and Enrico Ferri (1856-1929), proteges of Lombroso, completed the picture that was to serve as the forerunner for modern criminology. These two investigators advanced the concept that the criminal offender was in large part a social product, not altogether a free moral agent responsible for his acts and that in order to be understood, the forces in his environment, both internal and external (biological and social), that produced him must be scientifically explored and analyzed.*

Healy signalized the turning point in criminological research in the United States when he affirmed the principle of multiple causation in individual cases in contrast to deterministic theories of single causation for crime or criminals in general.† He brought into clearer focus the compound formula of human behavior and called attention to the kaleidoscopic interaction of biological forces in the individual with those of his environment. Healy's findings were confirmed by Burt in England and by others.‡ Medical experts, sociologists, psychologists, psychiatrists and other workers in the behavior sciences now generally recognize the union of the biological and social sciences as a necessary prerequisite to the scientific study of delinquent and criminal behavior.

Even Hooton, who stresses the anthropological aspects of crime and the criminal, was willing to concede the play of social pressures in the environment. He concluded that it is from the physically inferior element of the population that the native-born American criminals originate, and that such inferior stock gravitates to inferior environments. Thus, he takes

---

*Ferri, Enrico, *Criminal Sociology*, New York, D. Appleton-Century, 1896.

†Healy, William, *The Individual Delinquent*, Boston, Little, Brown, 1915, pp. 16, 33-125, 130-138.

‡Burt, Cyril, *The Young Delinquent*, New York, D. Appleton, 1938.

the position that criminality results from the impact of bad environment on "low grade" human organisms.° Likewise, the European school of criminal biology gives substantial recognition to environmental forces in the etiology of delinquent and criminal behavior.

During the past quarter century, the literature of criminology, including the prodigious works of Eleanor and Sheldon Glueck, has expanded at a rapidly increasing rate. It is concerned almost completely with a shift in emphasis toward the prevention of delinquency and crime and the rehabilitation of offenders who have already made their contact with the law, rather than with punishment as a tool of reformation and control.

As will be seen presently, the facts speak for themselves, and with considerable eloquence.

° Hooton, Arnest, *The American Criminal: An Anthropological Study*, Cambridge, Harvard, 1939, pp. 304-309.

Chapter 3

TOWARD PREVENTION

W HEN THE history of the American police is written, the past four decades will be recorded as the era of scientific crime detection. During this period almost unbelievable advances have been made in the application of scientific disciplines to investigative procedure. Prompt case solutions have become a matter of routine with the increased range of skills of the trained police officer and detective.

All of the arts and sciences have been brought into play in the detection and apprehension of the criminal and the production of evidence against him. At the convenient disposal of the investigator are the miracles of physics, chemistry, the microscope, the spectroscope, the metalloscope, photography, microphotography and other scientific facilities for the laboratory analysis and identification of questioned materials involved as evidence in criminal cases.

Circumstantial evidence has come into its own. Witness the difference between acquittal and a penitentiary sentence in an aggravated rape case which pivoted upon the technical laboratory identification of a small particle of evidence not much larger than the period at the end of this sentence. The attacker enticed his victim, a young girl eight years of age, into his car and then drove to a secluded spot in a thickly wooded area near the outskirts of a western city. The crime was completed with all the viciousness and brutality that a thirty-six-year-old degenerate could summon for the occasion.

Following the girl's release from a hospital a week later, she was able to lead the officers to the scene. Unidentifiable tire tracks were in evidence but it was noted that at fender height. the bark had been scraped from a number of young trees. On one of these exposed surfaces an officer discovered a small fleck of foreign substance which apparently did not belong to the tree.

With the care and precision of a man trained for police service, he recovered this small bit of evidence and promptly turned it over to the laboratory for examination. A standard sample of paint was taken from the right front fender of a suspect's car which showed that it had brushed against an object. Through micro-chemical and spectrographic analysis, it was identified with mathematical certainty as paint from the right front fender of the suspect's car. The defendant had previously made it clear with considerable emphasis in a signed statement that no one but himself ever drove the car in question. The task of the jury was comparatively simple.

In a fatal hit-and-run case, six fibers recovered from a suspected car were identified as coming from a gray woolen sweater worn by an elderly man at the time he was struck down and killed. Confronted with this evidence the suspected driver who showed a high blood alcohol concentration, made a detailed confession which he further confirmed the following morning.

Typical of the professional gains that have been made by the police was the prompt solution of an extortion case in Berkeley, California, several years ago—solved by a piece of string which tied together six sticks of dynamite. Laboratory analysis of residue recovered by centrifuge from fibers in this string revealed that the lethal package probably came from a farm on which would be found a sorrel horse, a Jersey cow, black and white rabbits, pine trees, several varieties of rare plants, Rhode Island Red chickens, and a fast-running stream of water. This incredible store of information extracted from a piece of string shortened the investigative trail which led to the men who had stolen the dynamite and who were parties to this threat against a man's life.

Such instances are now legion in the annals of the American police. The trained officer and detective supported as they are today by the technical resources of the laboratory, present an almost invincible combination in the investigation of crime. The era of scientific crime detection has witnessed the virtual extinction of the so-called crime mystery. From the records we are compelled to conclude that the American police have been doing an outstanding job of law enforcement.

With the investigative resources now at the disposal of the police, the criminal cases reported to them for investigation are in large part being solved and the offenders are being jailed and booked for trial. Statistics covering admissions to penitentiaries, reformatories, jails, training schools and releases on probation reveal a convincing measure of success being achieved by trial machinery, including the police and the prosecution, in obtaining convictions.

In fact, the police have been catching juvenile and adult offenders and processing them at such a level of efficiency that public institutions in this country are now crowded far beyond their capacity. The judge of one juvenile court in a western city recently had two hundred youngsters, tried and convicted, awaiting admission to the state reformatory. The fact that institutional facilities are lacking to accommodate the end result is beside the point. The conclusion remains that police administration in the United States has established an unequalled record of performance in the application of enforcement *as an instrument of crime control.*

With the total resources of the administration of justice in this country geared to enforcement and the punitive function, the American people and the police have become aware of the utter futility of this approach to the number one social problem. Enforcement has been given a fair trial! It has not produced the results anticipated by a society that has worshipped at the shrine of punishment as the major strategy.

Public opinion is now beginning to evaluate information that has been known to the police in every community for many years. Police administrators know that despite their best efforts, it is true that no reduction has been noted in the available crime statistics of this country. In fact, if we accept the criminal case loads of police departments as a guide in measuring criminality in the United States, the conclusion is inescapable that crime has been increasing at a consistent rate for the past fifty years and during the last two decades as indicated previously—more than ten times faster than the rate of population increase.

This discouraging fact has prompted the police to look in other directions for more effective measures of control. In casting about for a solution, recognition has long since gained foothold in police circles that the jail, the reformatory and the penitentiary must be supported and augmented by a strong preventive effort out in the community to the end that this needless sacrifice of life and its important values may be reduced to more acceptable dimensions.

It is obvious that crime detection and the apprehension of criminal offenders must go on. A bank is robbed; a child is kidnapped; a citizen is murdered. Immediate action is imperative. The offender must be caught, the kidnapper apprehended and the murderer taken into custody. No intelligent person can question the necessity of this immediate program in which the police, the prosecutor, the judge and correctional officials all play a vital and fundamental role.

But the futility of the manhunt as the total answer to the problem is apparent to every experienced police officer. After thirty-two years as America's outstanding chief of police, August Vollmer, noted police consultant and criminologist, stated: "I have spent my life enforcing the laws. It is a stupid procedure and has not, nor will it ever, solve the problem unless it is supplemented by preventive measures."*

After the home has failed; after the school has failed; and after the church, neighborhood and community have failed; the police are called in to make the arrest and somehow in a punitive scheme of things, to effect a dramatic change in the direction of a life pattern. The enforcement process is not prepared very well for the alteration of human behavior and the youngster in too many instances becomes involved in a more serious infraction of the law and is sent to the reformatory where society once again expects the miracle to be performed.

Despite our best efforts at reformation, the reformatory is too often the prelude to a penitentiary record. Correctional administration has made important professional gains in the past half century. Although workers in this area realize that a transforma-

---

*Leonard, V. A., *The Police of the 20th Century*, Brooklyn, Foundation Press, 1967, p. 84.

tion of temperament, personality and the behavior complex at this level in the individual's life presents a major challenge, encouraging progress is being made.

In terms of rehabilitation, so far as imprisonment and its substitutes—parole and probation—are concerned, it is difficult to escape the basic fact that firmly entrenched behavior patterns are the objects of reform. Habits of behavior and anti-social responses to the problems and situations of life have been conditioned over a long period of time in the individual's career and are extremely difficult to overcome. In the approach to this problem, it is to be noted that it is now possible to prepare for a career in the correctional field at the university level, with all this means in providing a calibre of personnel equal to the dimensions and challenge of the job.

On another vein, as early as 1937, Warden James A. Johnston of the Federal Penitentiary at Alcatraz, speaking on the functions of the modern prison, concluded, "Prisons have important work to perform. I want to see them bettered, improved, modernized and humanized. But when all is said and done, the finest prison that we can build will stand as a monument to neglected youth."* Walter Dunbar, Director of the California State Department of Corrections, observed, "We are trying to help the offender after his criminal pattern has developed. This is almost like waiting until a youth is crippled by polio to give him vaccine."†

THE JUVENILE DELINQUENT

Research in this country and abroad has largely confirmed the opinions held by the American police officer and detective for many years. The records of the police have long revealed that in the majority of cases, the adult criminal offender was on the

---

*Johnson, Warden James A., Federal Penitentiary at Alcatraz, *Functions of the Modern Prison*, quoted from an address delivered by Henry W. Wichofen, U. S. Assistant Attorney General, *The Police and Crime Prevention*, at the University of Illinois, June 17, 1937.

†Dunbar, Walter, *California Youth Quarterly*, vol. 16, no. 1, Spring, 1963.

march toward frustration and tragedy as a juvenile delinquent. Studies completed by such distinguished social scientists as William Healy and Augusta Bronner, Edwin H. Sutherland, Eleanor and Sheldon Glueck, Dr. Herman Adler and a host of others

CHART XI

Proposed Juvenile Justice System

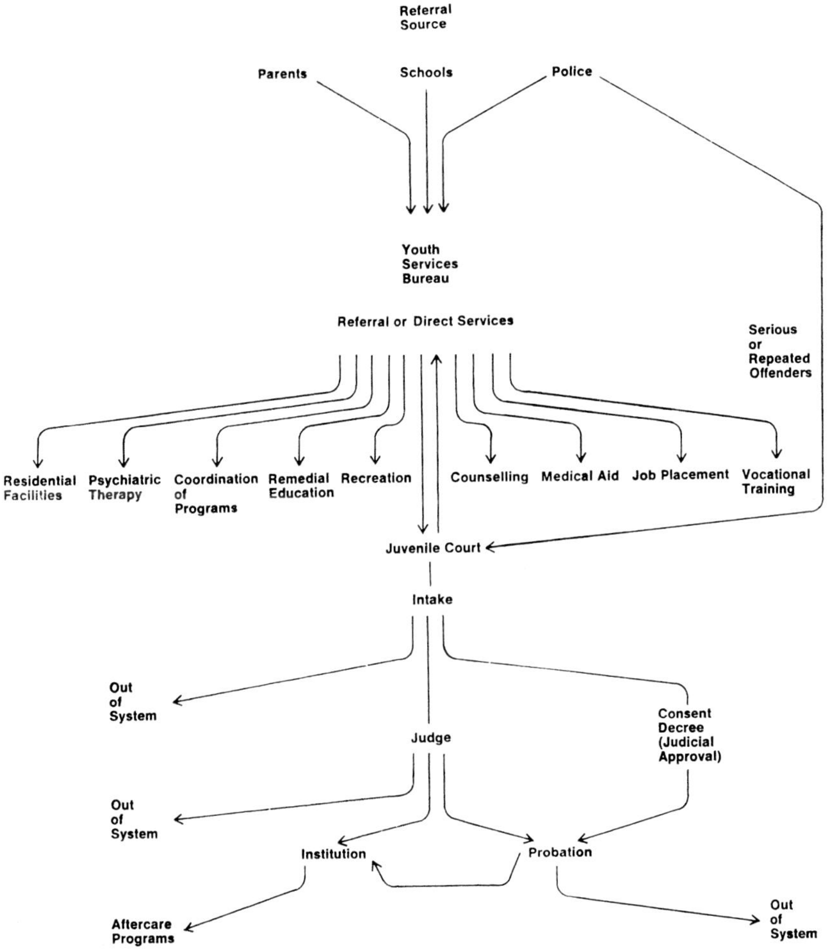

President's Commission on Law Enforcement and Administration of Justice, *The Challenge of Crime in a Free Society,* Washington, U. S. Government Printing Office, 1967, p. 89.

have shown that the officers were on firm ground in believing that the young delinquent was not likely to change his behavior pattern during adolescence and early manhood. That the young delinquent is the forerunner of the adult criminal offender has now been proven by the analysis of thousands of criminal careers.

The results of other research investigations have served to further confirm the verdict of the records in every American police department. Among others, Healy and Bronner concluded,* "Checking a delinquent career once started is no easy matter. In any treatment project, there is no royal road to success."

The evidence is conclusive in showing that where behavior disorders are permitted to develop unattended up to the point where the youngster knocks on the door at police headquarters for admission, the battle is almost lost. In fact, his presence in jail or the detention home for the first time is but a formality, the most recent of a chain of events in a conditioning process that has led to the end result.

The police in a leading midwestern city had searched for an experienced criminal ring. They arrested forty children. Sixteen were boys 15 years of age; fourteen were 14; five were 13; one was 12; two were 11; and two were 10. It is at this juncture in the development of a criminal career that society first springs heroically into action, and it is at this point that the enforcement and correctional process officially begins its record of failure.

It appears rational to believe that it is much better to attempt reform of the juvenile delinquent than to postpone action until the individual reaches maturity as a confirmed adult criminal offender. At the age level of juvenile delinquency, personality, temperament and behavior traits are still somewhat in the formative stage. They should be more accessible and responsive to the therapy of treatment than the adult offender with his fixed behavior patterns. Every available resource should, therefore, be applied toward the reclamation of as many youngsters

---

*Healy, William, and Bronner, Augusta, *Delinquents and Criminals, Their Making and Unmaking*, New York, Macmillan, 1926, p. 212.

as possible at this stage in the development of a criminal career.

However disconcerting it may prove to be, the records of the police and evidence uncovered by research compel the admission that an all-out attack upon the problem at the age level of juvenile delinquency holds little promise of substantial gain in the reduction of crime. Carr early observed.[*]

> Just as the reformers of the early nineteenth century were driven back from the adult prison to the juvenile "prison," which ultimately became the reform school, the correctional school and then to the school for maladjusted children; and just as the believers in institutional treatment were ultimately driven to set up a new court to attack the problem in a different way, and then the court had to seek help from the psychiatric clinic, so *modern reappraisals of all these efforts drive us still back one further step toward the beginning of deviant behavior.* It is not enough to treat. Inefficient as the actual procedures in the correctional cycle may be, there seems to be little prospect that they can ever be made efficient enough to do the whole job that is needed. Back behind the personality that has broken the law there is always an *earlier* phase of that same personality that has *just begun to deviate.*

Apparently, it is to these beginning deviations and the determining factors which produce them that police administration, the public school system and other social agencies in the community must now address themselves in what appears to be a more realistic approach to the problem.

It is evident that in the past, society and the community have been dealing with the end result rather than with the conditioning factors which produce the delinquent and the criminal. Policies in the field of crime control bear a strong resemblance to those of the housewife who was so busy swatting the flies in the kitchen that she failed to notice the garbage cans outside the window where they were breeding by the thousands.

Studies indicate that in most instances, the juvenile delinquent of today could have been easily recognized and identified as a developing behavior problem case in the early days of childhood when behavior patterns were taking form.

[*]Carr, Lowell J., *Delinquency Control,* New York, Harper & Bros., 1941, p. 181.

THE PRE-DELINQUENT

It was police recognition of the early symptoms of delinquent behavior that prompted Chief August Vollmer of the Police Department in Berkeley, California, and Dr. Jau Don Ball, Berkeley psychiatrist, to organize an investigation of children in the Hawthorne grade school of that community in 1919.* This study involving 220 children was without doubt the first effort made in this country to discover the facts concerning delinquency trends in the primary grades. These 220 children were examined at the clinical level by Ball and his associates, and at the conclusion of their study it was revealed that twenty-two youngsters, 10 per cent of those examined, presented problems involving mental, physical or social difficulties. This led him to recommend that they should receive special treatment and direction. The recommended therapy never materialized.

These problem youngsters included in the original 10 per cent were selected for an intensive follow-up study fourteen years later. The result again confirmed the opinion of the police that society's effort to combat crime must begin at the high chair level rather than that of the electric chair. It was found that 90 per cent of these problem children were then in an institution, had been in an institution, had police records or were community problems of one form or another.

It was this study that first suggested the coordination of community facilities in the attack upon delinquency. In the 1920's, Chief Vollmer conceived the idea of forming a panel to conduct a survey of the public school population in Berkeley at the primary grade level. The objective was to identify those children with problems—social, mental or physical—so severe that in the opinion of the panel unless they were given expert individual attention, they would run afoul of the law. At the conclusion of the survey, it was found that 3.5 per cent of the students fell into this category.

Following this study, the group met from time to time at

---

*Vollmer, August, Pre-delinquency, *Journal of Criminal Law and Criminology*. Vol. 14, August, 1923, pp. 279-283.

irregular intervals and new members were added, including Dr.
J. V. Breitweiser of the University of California, and Dr. Virgil
Dixon, then head of the Department of Vocational Guidance and
Research in the Berkeley public school system. Ultimately,
these meetings came to be formalized and gave birth to the
Coordinating Council movement in the United States.

A number of years later a graduate student at the University
of California, Nathan Bodin,* chose for his thesis problem a

TABLE VIII

DISTRIBUTION OF REASONS FOR CLASSIFICATION AS PROBLEM CHILDREN

Problem	Total Occurrence		Male		Female	
(Reason for reference)	No.	%	No.	%	No.	%
Mental retardation (a)	63	27.9	35	28.7	28	26.9
Persistent lying	29	12.8	15	12.3	14	13.5
Emotional instability (b)	26	11.5	13	10.7	13	12.5
Incorrigibility (c)	24	10.6	17	13.9	7	6.7
Stealing (d)	23	10.2	17	13.9	6	5.8
Truancy	20	8.9	11	9.0	9	8.7
Sex difficulty (e)	16	7.1	1	.8	15	14.4
School retardation (f)	10	4.4	7	5.7	3	2.9
Cheating	5	2.2	2	1.7	3	2.9
Marked cruelty	4	1.8	2	1.7	2	1.9
Extreme reticence	3	1.3	1	.8	2	1.9
Obscene language	3	1.3	1	.8	2	1.9
Total frequency of occurrence	226	100.0	122	100.0	104	100.0

(a) By mental retardation is meant not only a low I.Q. but also the inability to
do regular class work (retarded at least two school years).
(b) This classification was considered to include temper outbreaks, impertinence,
fighting, bullying, teasing, and sulkiness.
(c) Particularly uncontrollable and constantly playing minor tricks.
(d) Stealing at school or outside of school.
(e) Heterosexual and homosexual activity; masturbation.
(f) At least two years retarded in school. School retardation did not necessarily
mean mental retardation. Six of the ten school-retarded children in the group
had an I.Q. over 100, and one had an I.Q. of 118. School retardation might
be due to such factors as poor physical health, poor home environment, or
unadjusted school life.

---

*Bodin, Nathan, Do problem children become delinquents and criminals? con-
densed from a Master of Arts thesis, *Journal of Criminal Law and Criminology*,
November-December, 1936, pp. 545-559.

follow-up study to determine what had become of 116 adult persons who were considered by their teachers as definitely unadjusted when they were in the primary grades. They were considered problem children because for one reason or another they were nonconformists and "could not be satisfactorily managed in the regular school classroom." Table VIII indicates the distribution of the underlying reasons for which these 116 youngsters were considered problem children.

TABLE IX

DISTRIBUTION OF CRIMINAL OFFENSES AMONG 86 PROBLEM
CHILDREN EIGHT YEARS (AVERAGE) AFTER THEIR
IDENTIFICATION AS BEHAVIOR PROBLEM
CASES IN THE PRIMARY GRADES.

Offense	Total Arrests		Male		Female	
	No.	%	No.	%	No.	%
Larceny (except auto theft)	90	18.8	78	20.0	12	12.9
Burglary—breaking and entering	41	8.5	41	10.5	.....	.....
Robbery	11	2.3	11	2.8	.....	.....
Auto theft	8	1.7	8	2.1	.....	.....
Aggravated assault	3	.6	3	.8	.....	.....
Rape	1	.6	3	.8	.....	.....
Criminal homicide	1	.2	1	.3	.....	.....
Incorrigible and disorderly	76	15.9	43	11.0	33	35.4
Malicious mischief	61	12.7	58	14.9	3	3.2
Violation mun. police regulations	48	10.0	46	11.9	2	2.2
Sex offenses (excluding rape)	33	6.8	8	2.1	25	26.9
Disturbing the peace	32	6.6	27	6.9	5	5.4
Traffic and liquor violations	32	6.6	32	8.2	.....	.....
Violation of probation and parole	16	3.3	13	3.3	3	3.2
Attempted suicide	5	1.0	2	.5	3	3.2
Passing fictitious checks—forgery	4	.8	2	.5	2	2.2
Assault and battery	2	.4	2	.5	.....	.....
Failure to provide (for wife and/or child)	2	.4	1	.3	1	1.1
Extortion	1	.2	1	.3	.....	.....
Miscellaneous (a)	9	1.9	5	1.3	4	4.3
Unknown (b)	4	.8	4	1.0	.....	.....
Total	482	100.0	389	100.0	93	100.0

(a) Includes certification of insanity; reports for epileptic seizures; fugitive from justice; failure to appear in court; deserting navy.

(b) Includes those cases of violation of probation or parole where the actual offense was unknown.

The follow-up investigation by Bodin resulted in securing information on 93 of the 116 cases which he undertook to study. He found that 86 of these persons or 92 per cent were then in jail or had acquired delinquent and criminal records. Identified by their teachers in the primary grades as high social risks and flying the danger signals of impending delinquency and crime, behavior patterns developed uninterrupted and they joined the criminal ranks. Table X gives the distribution of offenses among the 92.5 per cent of these problem children who had by this time gone overboard in an abortive solution to life's problems.

The classifications in Table VIII are essentially in agree-

TABLE X

FREQUENCY OF OCCURRENCE OF VARIOUS TRAITS POSSESSED BY 874 PROBLEM CHILDREN IN THE PUBLIC SCHOOLS OF CLEVELAND.

Desire for Approval	%	*Reactions of Disinterest*	%
Tattling	42.0	Whispering	74.7
Cheating	29.5	Inattentive	59.0
Lying, untruthful	19.6	Careless work	44.4
Acting smart	14.6	Disorderly	38.8
Imaginative tales	13.3	Failure to study	36.2
Meddlesome	12.6	Daydreaming	33.4
Suggestible	9.4	Lack of interest	31.8
		Overactive	30.9
Reactions to Social Pressure	%	Neglectful	25.4
Shy, withdrawing	35.2	Physically lazy	20.8
Oversensitive	25.5	Unnecessary tardiness	17.6
Domineering	12.1	Slovenly	11.8
Fearful	9.3	*Reactions of Rebellion*	%
Coward	8.8		
Nervous	8.7	Interrupting	38.7
Quarrelsome	7.9	Overcritical	14.2
Unhappy, depressed	8.0	Sullen, sulky	12.5
Stubborn in group	7.5	Wilfully disobedient	8.2
Stealing articles	4.0	Destroying property	8.2
Sissy (or tomboy)	3.6	Rude, impudent	6.7
Cruel, bullying	1.7	Impertinent	5.6
Profanity	1.7	Carrying grudges	4.9
Stealing money	0.7	Truancy	1.6
Stealing food, sweets	0.7	Temper outbursts	1.5
Obscene notes, talk	0.3	*Physical Pleasures*	%
		Masturbation	3.9
		Enuresis	3.9
		Smoking	0.2

ment with the various traits possessed by problem children as reported by teachers for 874 Cleveland school children:*

Other studies have pointed out that delinquency and crime in the majority of cases stem from early life maladjustments, and that delinquent juveniles and adult criminals displayed in almost every case the symptoms of their future misconduct as early behavior problems.*

The philosophy of crime prevention flows from the conviction, now confirmed by research, that the burglar, killer, prostitute, automobile thief and stick-up do not become that way suddenly. The records show that in the majority of cases, they started their abortive development in early childhood and progressed by almost imperceptible degrees into confirmed criminal offenders. Early discovery, diagnosis and the application of therapeutic measures in behalf of the physically, mentally and socially different child are gradually opening the door to opportunities for the prevention of delinquency and crime which may overshadow the manhunt and the penitentiary.

A veteran jurist stated, "Messrs. Police Officers, Sheriffs and State Patrolmen: Do you want to meet the young killers, rapists, stick-ups, automobile thieves, burglars and others you will be chasing in a comparatively short time? If you do, go to the schools and look at the records that show the following information—chronic tardiness, persistent truancy, scholastic progress below mental ability, poor citizenship, unwillingness to accept correction and lack of interest. These records are red-flag warning signals of delinquency and crime and they will point you almost unerringly to your 'man.' "*

---

*Wickman, E. K., *Children's Behavior and Teacher's Attitudes*, Commonwealth Fund, Division of Publications, New York, 1928, pp. 232-233.

*Michal, J., and Adler, M. J., *An Institute of Criminology and Criminal Justice*, New York, 1923, p. 253.

Also see Glueck, Eleanor and Sheldon, *Delinquents and Nondelinquents in Perspective*, Cambridge, Harvard, 1968, as well as *Predicting Delinquency and Crime*, 1959, and *Unraveling Juvenile Delinquency*, 1951, by the same authors.

*Long, Honorable William G., Judge of the Seattle Juvenile Court. *The Relation of Juvenile Courts to Other Agencies*, Proceedings of the Fifth Pacific Northwest Law Enforcement Conference, Washington State University, Pullman, 1944, p. 26.

Addressing further comment to the teaching profession, he said, "Mr. and Mrs. School teacher—Would you like to do something for the public health of your community in the field of sick conduct? Then, heed your records. Under your very eyes are developing the symptoms of infection that will develop into the ruptured appendix or organic collapse of good citizenship. The attendance record alone is enough to put us all on guard."

THE PREDICTION OF DELINQUENCY

The foregoing brings into sharp relief the need for prediction mechanisms which will assist in identifying potential pre-delinquents in the first, second and third grades, and even at the nursery and kindergarten levels, so that the clinical resources of the school and the community can be brought into play in behalf of the youngster. The prediction criteria mentioned by Bodin and Judge Long have already been presented.

Prediction is nothing new. It has been around for years. State board examinations for admission to practice in medicine, law, engineering, pharmacy and the other professions; tests and examinations taken by the individual from the nursery through the Ph.D; projecting the crime and traffic accident curves of yesterday and today into tomorrow to determine what is going to happen, how much, when and where—are all matters of prediction. Other examples include the prediction of social adjustment, academic achievement, vocational interest and performance, and the outcome of marriage.

What is new is that prediction scales and techniques have been and continue to be the subject of extensive research and that they have become more sophisticated. A large body of literature is now available concerning attempts to predict human behavior in many areas of the individual's life. While it is true that as yet, no estimate of future behavior, arrived at by any means, can be made with mathematical certainty, *a statement of degree of probability is conceded to be an appropriate prediction objective.* This is entirely acceptable for the job at hand.

Suffice to say at this point that research thus far has made available prediction scales and techniques which to a very sub-

stantial degree satisfy this objective.* Predictive factors that
have been developed thus far by research workers, include the
following:

1. Discipline of child by father.
2. Supervision of child by mother.
3. Affection of father for child.
4. Affection of mother for child.
5. Cohesiveness of family.
   (Note—the foregoing five factors are presented in the Glueck's Prediction Scale.)
6. Social assertion.
7. Social defiance.
8. Suspicion.
9. Destructiveness.
10. Degree of emotional stability.
11. Stubbornness.
12. Running away.
13. Stealing.
14. Temper tantrums.
15. Disobedience.
16. Sex play.
17. Gambling.
18. Use of vile language.
19. Begging.
20. Staying out late at night.
21. Lying.
22. State of health.
23. Extrovert v. introvert.
24. Depression.
25. Complaining tendencies.
26. Results of psychological and psychiatric tests.
27. Reading ability.
28. Maladjustment.
29. Norm-violating behavior.
30. Objectionable personality traits.
31. Poor work habits.
32. Attitude toward schooling.
33. Attendance record and truancy.
34. Academic achievement level.

*Glueck, Sheldon and Eleanor, *Predicting Delinquency and Crime*, Cambridge, Harvard, 1959. President's Commission on Law Enforcement and Administration of Justice, *Task Force Report: Juvenile Delinquency and Youth Crime*, Washington, U. S. Gov. Print. Office, 1967, p. 171.

Glueck, Sheldon and Eleanor, *Delinquents and Non-delinquents in Perspective*, Cambridge, Harvard, 1968, p. 184.

Glueck, Sheldon and Eleanor, *Unraveling Juvenile Delinquency*, Harvard, 1951, pp. 15, 257-271, 284, 288.

*Amos, William E., and Wellford, Charles F., *Delinquency Prevention, Theory and Practice*, Englewood Cliffs, Prentice-Hall, 1967, pp. 22-36.

MacIver, Robert M., *The Prevention and Control of Delinquency*, New York, Atherton Press, 1967, pp. 104-123.

Kvaraceus, William C., et al., *Delinquent Behavior, Principles and Practices*, Washington, N.E.A., 1959, pp. 32-51.

Stratton, John R., and Terry, Robert M., *Prevention of Delinquency: Problems and Programs*, New York, Macmillan, 1968, pp. 51-99.

Dailey, John T., *Evaluation of the Contribution of Special Programs in the Washington, D. C., Schools to the Prediction and Prevention of Delinquency*, Washington, U. S. Office of Education, 1966.

President's Commission on Law Enforcement and Administration of Justice, *The Challenge of Crime in a Free Society*, Washington, U. S. Gov. Print. Office, 1967, p. 71.

All authorities in the field agree that the identification of potential delinquents on or before entrance in school or soon thereafter would open the door for the application of diagnostic and therapeutic measures in a program geared to the philosophy of delinquency and crime prevention. They agree in addition, that to complacently sit by until certain manifestations of delinquency are in evidence is to further populate the arrest blotter.

There are those who feel that the classroom teacher is in a strong position to identify potential delinquents. As a trained observer, it is held that she sees the pupil over an extended period of time and comes to know him intimately, and she is in an advantageous position to identify those students who are in need of psychological, psychiatric or cultural support.*

Again, most observers hold that the major approach should be directed toward the individual youngster as the unit of practice.† A minority take the position that there is a movement away from individual prophylaxis to community treatment directed toward deviation pressures in the environment. They hold that delinquency in the final analysis is not a property of individuals or even of subcultures but a product of the social systems in which the individual and group become enmeshed. They indicate that the pressures that produce delinquency originate in these structures and should be regarded, not as the individual or group that exhibits a delinquent pattern, but as the social setting that gives rise to delinquency. They urge, therefore, that effective efforts to reduce and prevent delinquency must be directed at those social conditions.

Following this same line of reasoning, they suggest that the magnitude and significance of the problem call for alteration of conditions in the community that will reduce delinquency in the short run through the prevention of recidivism among present delinquents and first-time violations among those who are currently delinquency-prone—and that will prevent delin-

---

*Stratton, John R., and Terry, Robert M., *Prevention of Delinquency: Problems and Programs*, New York, Macmillan, 1968, pp. 84-99.

†See footnote on page 50.

quency in the long run through the reduction of deviation pressures in the environment that make some youth delinquency-prone in the first place.*

On the contrary, the Gluecks concluded as recently as 1968, that the external environment, including poverty and the slums, are less significant in generating delinquency and crime than the *biological endowments of the individual and parental influence during the formative years of early life.* They point out that the general environment contributes relatively little to an understanding of the individual's maladjustment to the demands of accepted social standards.† They add, however, and logically so, that the pathology of the environment, including poverty, the slums and other factors that retard social development toward a better life, demand man's best attention.

It is more than significant that the Gluecks and others are taking into account the biological endowment of the individual as a part of the etiology of delinquency and crime. The genes are taking their place in the literature of criminology. It is becoming respectable to recognize that human behavior is genetically as well as socially determined. Genetics is moving into a foreground position as a member of the behavior sciences. The genes, holding as they do the blueprint for height, weight, color of eyes, hair, temperament, emotional bent, personality and other traits, are commanding the attention of workers in the field of criminology.‡

The Gluecks observe that, with respect to genetic endowment, little can be done presently in view of the general attitude toward the subject and the need for additional data in the

---

*Cloward, Richard A., and Ohlin, Lloyd E., *Delinquency and Opportunity*, New York, Free Press, 1960, p. 211.

President's Commission on Law Enforcement and Administration of Justice, *Task Force Report: Juvenile Delinquency and Youth Crime*, Washington, U. S. Gov. Print. Office, 1967, p. 223.

†Glueck, Sheldon and Eleanor, *Delinquents and Nondelinquents*, Cambridge, Harvard, 1968, p. 171.

‡Osborn, Frederick, *The Future of Human Heredity*, New York, Weybright and Talley, 1969.

biological sciences. There is some evidence, however, that the educational process is making itself felt in this area. The increasing number of genetic counseling centers across the United States is of more than ordinary interest.

Virtually all authorities in the field concede that the home, the school and the church occupy commanding positions in the total project of delinquency and crime prevention. Strangely enough, the opinion is not entirely unanimous concerning the church and this apparent paradox will be considered in some detail. It appears relevant to consider the role of all three of these major social institutions.

THE HOME

The broken home—by death, discord or divorce—showed in a number of studies twice the average rate of delinquency. In the presence of strong family cohesiveness, delinquency rates are below average. It has been held that the stability and continuity of family life stand out as a most important factor in the development of the child. Monahan is of the view that the strengthening and preserving of normal family life could probably accomplish more in the prevention of delinquency than any other program yet devised.*

The noted delinquency prediction scale developed by the Gluecks is based entirely on the home, referred to by some as "under the roof culture." The scale is worth repeating at this point.

1. Discipline by father.
2. Supervision by mother.
3. Affection on the part of father.
4. Affection on the part of mother.
5. Cohesiveness of family.†

Carr observes that where a family departs from structural

---

*Giallombardo, Rose, *Juvenile Delinquency, A Book of Readings*, New York, John Wiley & Sons, 1966, pp. 209-221.

†Glueck, Sheldon and Eleanor, *Predicting Delinquency and Crime*, Cambridge, Harvard, 1951.

completeness (both parents in home), racial homogeneity, economic security, cultural conformity, moral conformity, physical and psychological normality and functional adequacy, to that extent, it operates as a negative deviation pressure on the child.*

The President's Commission had this to say:† "The programs and activities of almost every kind of social institution with which children come in contact—schools, churches, social service agencies, youth organizations—are predicated on the assumption that children acquire their fundamental attitudes toward life, their moral standards, in their homes."

The family is the first and most basic institution in our society for developing the child's potential, in all its many aspects— emotional, intellectual, moral and spiritual, as well as physical and social. Other influences do not even enter the child's life until after the first few highly formative years. It is within the family that the child must learn to curb his desires and to accept rules that define the time, place and circumstances under which highly personal needs may be satisfied in socially acceptable ways. This early training—management of the emotions, confrontation with rules and authority, development of responsiveness to others—has been repeatedly related to the presence or absence of delinquency in later years. But cause-and-effect relationships have proven bewilderingly complex and require much more clinical experience and systematic research.

Research findings, however, while far from conclusive, point to the principle that whatever in the organization of the family diminishes the moral and emotional authority of the family in the life of the young person also increases the likelihood of delinquency.

More crucial even than mode of discipline is the degree of parental affection or rejection of the child. Perhaps the most important factor in the lives of many boys who become delin-

---

*Carr, Lowell J., *Delinquency Control*, New York, Harper & Bros., 1941, p. 112.
†President's Commission on Law Enforcement and Administration of Justice, *The Challenge of Crime in a Free Society*, Washington, U. S. Print. Office, 1967, p. 6.

quent is their failure to win the affection of their fathers. It has been suggested that delinquency correlates more with the consistency of the affection the child receives from both parents than with the consistency of the discipline. It has also been found that a disproportionately large number of aggressive delinquents have been denied the opportunity to express their feelings of dependence on their parents."

Healy and Bronner° found that the extent to which immediate surroundings in home life affect the chances for normal development or for reformation is always a very pertinent inquiry in the individual case.

It has been freely conceded that the family is the primary social institution responsible for raising children. The implications are quite plain in terms of the home communicating to the child the basic values and standards of society.†

Gault reported early that the conclusions of researchers supported the common-sense view that in the nature of the home and the neighborhood are to be found the primary roots of criminal careers and the primary defense against their development. He points out the obvious that in every case, the criminal man or woman was a child before he became a criminal offender and that it was in the home with the persons of father and mother that the individual made his initial contacts.‡ In connection with the far-reaching influence upon the youngster of the home and home life, Bernard Shaw made this interesting observation, "The only occupation for which no training is required is parenthood."§

THE SCHOOL

It has been observed that norm-violating behavior develops over a fairly long period of time. The important implication of

°Healy, William and Bronner, Augusta F., *Delinquents and Criminals, Their Making and Unmaking*, New York, Macmillan, 1926, p. 117.

†Kvaraceus, William C., *et al.*, *Delinquent Behavior*, Washington, N.E.A., 1959, p. 224.

‡Gault, Robert H., *Criminology*, New York, D. C. Heath, 1932, p. 406.

§Robison, Sophia, *Juvenile Delinquency*, New York, Holt, Rinehart and Winston, 1960, p. 69.

this is that the school, more particularly the classroom teacher who has the opportunity of observing the youngster over an extended period of time, is in a strong position to detect and identify those who are in need of emotional, psychological or cultural support. It goes without saying that if identification of the pre-delinquent can be made in the early grades, the school and the community can bring their total effort to bear upon the youngster and his problems with a strong certainty that the development of delinquent behavior can be forestalled.*

An extensive study of the public school population in Washington, D. C., revealed that the juvenile crime rate in each local neighborhood of the District of Columbia was significantly related to the percentage of poor readers in the elementary schools serving a particular neighborhood. It was found that when the 90 per cent poor reader mark is reached, the crime rate increases at a sharply accelerating rate. The study emphasized the high correlation between delinquent behavior and poor reading ability.†

The President's Commission had this to say concerning the relation between failure in school and delinquency:

> When the school system is not adequately equipped to meet the early learning problems a child brings to school with him, a cycle of deterioration and failure may be set in motion. As the youngster is promoted from grade to grade to keep him with his age mates but before he has really mastered his tasks, failure becomes cumulative.
>
> The child, in self-defense, reacts against the school, perhaps openly rebelling against its demands. He and others like him seek each other out. Unable to succeed in being educated, they cannot afford to admit that education is important. Unwilling to accept the school's humiliating evaluation of them, they begin to flaunt its standards and reject its long-range goals in favor of conduct more immediately gratifying.

---

*Kvaraceus, William C., *et al.*, Washington, *Delinquent Behavior*, Washington, N.E.A., 1959, p. 32. This book is especially recommended to police personnel.
†Dailey, John T., *Evaluation of the Contribution of Special Programs in the Washington, D. C., Schools to the Prediction and Prevention of Delinquency*, Washington, An educational research project at the George Washington University, August, 1966.

That conduct may not at first be seriously delinquent, but it represents a push toward more destructive and criminal patterns of behavior. Moreover, it takes forms such as repeated truancy; it may land to dropping out of school. Both common sense and research data support the view that the high degree of correlation between delinquency and failure in school is more than accidental.

Flexible school administrative arrangements would make it possible to assign difficult students to regular classes taught by teachers who are particularly successful with such students. Teacher seminars would enable those teachers to share their insights with their fellows.

A number of experimental methods of dealing with misbehavior problems show promise. Some give added responsibilties to problem children. Other programs have improved school performance and reduced misbehavior in class with group techniques. Some schools have initiated and had favorable experience with efforts to detect delinquent tendencies at the elementary school level and to deal with them in a variety of ways, including special inservice training for teachers, special counselors and social services, incentive and reward systems for pupils and cooperative work with parents.°

Carr states that the public school as one agency that deals with 90 per cent of the children of the United States bears an especially heavy responsibility in delinquency control and prevention.† Kvaraceus observes that the schools occupy a commanding position in a community program for the prevention and control of juvenile delinquency. Children enter school at an early period of life when behavior patterns are just beginning to take form and a real opportunity is presented to assist them in becoming well-integrated and socially useful citizens. He further makes the point that they have a tactical advantage enjoyed by no other agency concerned with the prevention of delinquency and crime.‡

The police and the public school represent the two major social agencies coming into contact with the youngsters of the

---

°President's Commission on Law Enforcement and Administration of Justice, *The Challenge of Crime in a Free Society*, Washington, U. S. Print. Office, 1967, p. 71.

†Carr, Lowell J., *Delinquency Control*, New York, Harper & Bros., 1941, p. 360.

‡Kvaraceus, William C., *The Community and the Delinquent*, Yonkers-on-Hudson, World Book Company, 1954, p. 265.

community. For this reason, the police should make a special effort to develop a close working relationship with the schools, including school counselors and guidance officers. In this connection, police personnel would find it advantageous to obtain a copy of *A Guide for Cooperation Between School Officials and the Police,* prepared and published by the Pennsylvania Department of Public Instruction, Harrisburg, Pennsylvania.

THE CHURCH

In the control and prevention of delinquency and crime, the church occupies a commanding position as one of the major social institutions in organized society. By its very nature, it should be one of the greatest constructive forces available to man.

A survey of the works of leading authorities in the field of criminology revealed a divided opinion with respect to the impact of the church on the prevention of delinquency and crime. Some emphasize the crime prevention role of religion; others attach little importance to the contributions of the church; there are even those who identify religion as a causal factor in delinquency and crime; still others take an intermediate position.*

Thorndyke, in his study of 310 cities above 30,000 population, was unable to establish any correlation between the "goodness" score of a community and any objective measurement of church activity or membership.†

The President's Commission observes:

> Many organizations already exist that have as one of their aims, if not the major one, the provision of programs for young people. Perhaps most universal are religious institutions, many of which offer a wide variety of services ranging from individual counseling

---

*Taft, Donald R., *Criminology,* New York, Macmillan, 1943, p. 213-214.

†Thorndyke, E. L., *Your City,* New York, Harcourt, Brace, 1939, p. 62—a penetrating discussion in which this researcher attempts to formulate a measuring scale for determining the desirability of any given community as a place in which to live and raise a family.

to group activities, from traditional religious instruction and worship to outward-looking community improvement efforts.

The important contribution churches, synagogues, and other religious institutions can make to crime prevention is evident. They are leading exponents and guardians of the community's moral and ethical standards. They have the ability to understand and teach in their largest context the great principles of honesty and honor, of compassion and charity, of respect and reverence that underlie not only the Nation's laws but its entire being. They have the power to move men's spirits and sway their minds.*

Carr expressed concern over what he regarded as the failure of the church to utilize its full potential and urged a greater involvement of church organization and membership out in the community, including close contact with social agencies, close inter-church cooperation, a direct working relationship with the schools in treating problem cases, both predelinquent and delinquent, and the providing of guidance counseling for boys and girls in trouble.†

Dr. George R. Mursell, at one time psychologist of the Ohio Department of Welfare, in a study of a reform school population, found that the inmates had received as much religious training as had the children outside. He came to the conclusion that there was in general no significant relationship between religious training and delinquent or non-delinquent behavior.‡

The foregoing evaluations of the church by authorities in the field of delinquency and crime prevention would seem to indicate a disturbing degree of impotence on the part of the church in the approach to this major social problem. However, some exceptions to these opinions must be put into the record.

Referring again to the Glueck's delinquency prediction scale, it will be noted that they developed five factors, all concerned

---

*President's Commission on Law Enforcement and Administration of Justice, *The Challenge of Crime in a Free Society*, Washington, U. S. Gov. Print. Office, 1967, p. 68 and 290.

†Carr, Lowell J., *Delinquency Control*, New York, Harper and Bros., 1941, pp. 369-362.

‡Teeters, Negley K., and Reinemann, John Otto, *The Challenge of Delinquency*, New York, Prentice-Hall, 1950, p. 159.

with the home, which indicated to them whether a youngster was being conditioned for a normal, successful life, or as a candidate for the jail, juvenile court, reformatory, and ultimately the penitentiary. They bear repeating:

1. Discipline by father.
2. Supervision by mother.
3. Affection of father.
4. Affection of mother.
5. Cohesiveness of family.

All of these basic elements are supported by the doctrine of Christianity and in the majority of homes in this country, it appears safe to assume that its influence finds important expression through these factors in family life as a whole.

The following note by an anonymous writer, to which most Americans would subscribe, would seem to indicate that it hardly would be correct to underestimate the influence of the church in human affairs.*

One Solitary Life

He was born in an obscure village, the child of a peasant woman. He grew up in still another village, where he worked in a carpenter shop until he was thirty. Then for three years he was an itinerant preacher. He never wrote a book. He never held office. He never had a family or owned a home. He didn't go to college. He never visited a big city.

He never traveled two hundred miles from the place where he was born. He did none of the things one usually associates with greatness. He had no credentials but himself. He was only thirty-three when the tide of public opinion turned against him. His friends ran away.

He was turned over to his enemies and went through the mockery of a trial. He was nailed to a cross between two thieves. While he was dying, his executioners gambled for his clothing, the only property he had on earth. When he was dead, he was laid in a borrowed grave, through the pity of a friend.

Nineteen centuries have come and gone, and today he is the central figure of the human race and the leader of mankind's progress. All the armies that ever marched, all the navies that ever sailed, all the parliaments that ever sat, all the kings that ever reigned, put to-

---

The Denton Record-Chronicle, Editorial page, December 24, 1969.

gether, have not affected the life of man on this earth as much as
that one solitary life.

Nevertheless, the opinions presented in the foregoing pages
do bear the stamp of some authority and present a challenge
of important proportions to all concerned. Carr's recommendations would seem to be particularly relevant.

It is intended that the materials presented in the first three
chapters serve as a foundation for the approach to police crime
prevention. They draw the dimensions of the problem of delinquency and crime and, as far as space permits, provide an
overview of the measures society has taken thus far in the
direction of regulation, control and prevention. They provide
an appropriate setting and introduction to the ensuing chapters
which are devoted exclusively to the police role in the total
project of delinquency and crime prevention.

FIGURE 1. Not an unusual sight: The Chief of Police and his officers,
except those on stand-by, in the police department of Owosso, Michigan,
pause just before entering the church on Easter Sunday. (Reproduced
through the courtesy of the Owosso Police Department.)

Chapter 4

THE POLICE ROLE

DELEGATED as society's first line of defense against crime and the criminal, the police occupy a commanding position in this advance upon the crime problem. Police administration has the machinery and the methods to focus the community's attack on crime—upstream at the source.

The police conduct an around-the-clock operation. They have a mobile personnel which moves rapidly and as a matter of routine into areas where all other agencies in the community would find unhampered movement difficult. They have the power of the State behind them.

Due to the very nature of their work, the police are more familiar than any other organized group with the crime hazards in the community that play their part in the needless wreckage of human life. They are in a position to understand the criminal and the forces which result in his development. They have in their files the basic records data and information concerning delinquency and crime that are necessary for an intelligent plan of operation.

Because the police and the public schools are generally the first to have official contact with a child both before and after he has gotten into trouble, theirs is an opportunity presented to no other branch of government. Developing delinquency cases and the conditioning factors that produce them come under their observation long before other social agencies are aware of them. The number of children who reach the juvenile court, or who are committed to institutions, represent but a fraction of the total number of borderline youngsters contacted by the police and school authorities.

More important, however, is the fact that the police operate under a direct mandate from the people to achieve crime control. Organized police service represents society's basic defense against crime and the criminal. There is no substitute. The law is plain in outlining the responsibility of police administration as the primary agency of social control in the repression of crime and disorder.

This mandate to the police carries with it the obligations of leadership. The attack upon crime is primarily an administrative problem of local government in coordinating the forces and resources of the community under centralized direction and supervision. It is manifest that all major effort in the direction of crime control, whether enforcement or prevention, must pivot on local police administration. O. W. Wilson, formerly Dean of the School of Criminology at the University of California and later Superintendent of the Chicago Police Department, has pointed out that the best intentions of the various social service agencies and institutions in the community will not result in any substantial progress toward the solution of the problem unless their efforts are guided and directed by the police.*

Again, in the second edition of his work, *Police Administration,* he emphasizes that the police department is the logical agency in local government to set in motion and coordinate the efforts of all other agencies and groups and give direction to their combined approach in the total project of delinquency and crime prevention.†

No longer is the American chief of police content to dispose of inquiries concerning crime and delinquency in his community with the comment, "no problem here." He is frank to concede without hesitation that "there is a problem here," because he knows that his community is producing its proportionate share of crime and criminals. He knows that it is not enough to realize that his organization is undermanned and

---

*Wilson, O. W. (Dean of the School of Criminology, University of California), *Police crime prevention activity, American Journal of Medical Jurisprudence,* Vol. 2, January, 1939, p. 2.

†Wilson, O. W., *Police Administration,* 2nd ed., New York, McGraw-Hill, 1963, p. 328.

that the crime caseload of his department argues against assuming any additional responsibilities; rather, it argues for him to do so.

It is evident to him that vice raids and other necessary expressions of enforcement are not the total answer, and that fines, bail bonds, trial, conviction and the penitentiary are trademarks of failure in the effort to reduce crime. He is aware of the circumstance that virtually every time one of his scout cars answers a call, its destination is some social problem. Working forever at the explosive center of behavior situations and with the conditions that produce them, the chief of police and his personnel are in a strong position to play a commanding role in the preventive approach to these problems. This man who heads one of the nation's police forces, small or large, will certify that the content of the arrest blotter is largely the end-result of failure on the part of the home, the school, the church and other socially constructive forces in the community. The challenge to the police and the people they serve is unmistakable.

POLICE ORGANIZATION FOR DELINQUENCY PREVENTION

The prevention of delinquency and crime is a fundamental responsibility of the patrol force. The preventive role of the individual patrolman is a basic element of modern police service. The mere presence of a properly organized and efficiently operating patrol force is conceded to be one of the greatest crime deterrents at the disposal of organized society.

Patrol Beat Responsibility

The compelling requirement or prerequisite for the effective use of the patrol force in this important area of the police operation is a determination of policy by police management with respect to *patrol beat responsibility*, especially in the smaller department. Everything pivots on this determination.

Policy in regard to this critical decision will vary from one department to another. At one end of the administrative spectrum, the detective is charged with total investigative responsibility. The patrolman merely responds to the radio call, makes an arrest, if perchance this is possible, and protects the scene until the detectives arrive to launch the investigation.

Under this ill-advised policy, the detective unit usually finds itself overloaded with uncleared cases in every category, with the result that major crime fails to receive the attention that it deserves, and the patrolman has relatively little to do. With little or no investigative responsibility, there is little or no incentive for the individual patrolman to exercise his potential capabilities in the prevention of delinquency and crime. It is difficult to escape the observation that under this arrangement, the department experiences a tragic waste of manpower because of the unused resources of the patrol force—this, despite the sobering fact that patrol salaries represent the largest single item in the police budget.

There follows in succession those departments where the patrol officer is held responsible for the preliminary investigation of cases originating on his beat and the filing of a report covering his investigative activities on the case. The follow-up investigation and final clearance or disposition are a responsibility of the detective, except perhaps in minor cases.

At the other end of the spectrum is the department operating under a policy where virtually total case investigation and case clearance responsibility are assigned to the officer on the beat. Under this administrative concept, the officer is responsible for the investigation and clearance of all cases originating on his beat, regardless of classification.

He is geared to the total delivery of police service, which means that he is held responsible for the robbery rate, the burglary rate, the automobile theft rate, the amount of grand and petty larceny, the extent of juvenile delinquency, the number of traffic accidents, traffic congestion, and all other police problems that originate within the limits of the patrol area to which he is assigned. All uncleared cases represent a direct charge against the efficiency of the individual patrolman concerned and provide a fair index to his general performance record. Referred to by some as the "all purpose patrolman," and by Bristow as the "Generalist,"* he is totally responsible for the case investigation and its final disposition in all of these categories.

The following significant paragraph appears in the general information bulletin for applicants furnished by one police department to potential candidates for the position of patrolman before an application form is issued:

> A patrolman is responsible for all crimes or reports arising on his beat. The officer reports off his beat after completing his tour of duty, and is then required to write reports on all cases handled by him. This may take only a few minutes, or it may take several hours, depending upon the nature of the cases handled and the ability of the individual. Patrolmen are held responsible for the investigation of all complaints regardless of seriousness and regardless of the fact that detectives or other officers may assist and counsel in the investigation.

Obviously, the individual patrolman cannot discharge all of these duties and responsibilities without considerable assistance from others, and for this reason, he has at his disposal the entire resources of the department. The facilities of the detective unit or in any jurisdiction where the position of detective has been abolished or not yet created, experienced patrolmen in plain clothes are available to give the necessary assistance in the investigation of felony cases or in other instances where the case investigation would take the officer beyond the boundaries of his beat.

Members of the prevention unit likewise come to his assistance in the solution of problems associated with the prevalence of juvenile delinquency in the area to which he is assigned. Similarly, the facilities of the crime laboratory, whether it is a local, state or national facility, the records unit, the vice officer or officers, and all other administrative units in the organization cooperate with the individual patrolman in keeping his beat clean.

But regardless of the type or volume of assistance he may

---

*Bristow, Allen P., *Effective Police Manpower Utilization*, Springfield, Thomas, 1969, p. 18.

bring into play, he cannot "pass the buck"; the responsibility for the delivery of police service in that area to which he is assigned belongs exclusively to him. Such a system requires a superior man in police uniform, superior recruiting standards, and a superior training program, together with a salary structure that will attract this type of personnel. Today, this is the calibre of manpower that is being recruited on an increasing scale into the American police services.*

At this point, further comment concerning the detective unit appears to be relevant. The primary function of the detective is to apprehend those offenders who escape arrest at the hands of the patrol force, and the recovery of stolen property. In the growth of a police department, the necessity may eventually arise for the creation of the position of detective, when the un-cleared caseload of the patrol force reaches a point where de-partmental efficiency indicates the need for specialized assis-tance. Numerous offenses come to the attention of the police which require extensive investigation both in time and place for their solution. Thus, the number of these offenses and the grave character of many of them may, in the course of time, make necessary the organization of a separate unit in the de-partment manned by persons assigned exclusively to criminal investigation.

In the larger departments, specialization develops within the detective unit or division. Such specialization permits the in-vestigator to concentrate his time and energies in the investiga-tion of a particular type of criminal activity. Through con-tinuous work in a specific criminal area, he gradually builds up a fund of skills and information which contributes to his capability and performance and that of the department.

He comes to know personally the offenders who operate within the specific criminal specialty which constitutes the functional area assigned to him for investigation. He becomes familiar with their methods of operation or *modus operandi*,

---

*Leonard, V. A., *Police Patrol Organization* (for the smaller department), Springfield, Thomas, 1970.

their habits, friends, relatives and close associates. Not infrequently, an experienced detective is able to narrow the investigation and search down to a single individual after a careful study of the crime scene and recognition of the salient features of the *modus operandi*.

As a result of the yield from specialization in criminal investigation, detective divisions, particularly in the larger cities, are decentralized functionally into special details, such as the homicide, robbery, burglary, automobile theft, worthless check, bunco, and other specialized squads. Caseload volume usually determines the necessity for the creation of a specialized squad. Such units should be created only in response to a real need and they should be liquidated or consolidated with another unit when the need has passed or ceased to be acute or continuous.

Here again, detective units are manned by transfers from the patrol force, backbone of a police organization, with a corresponding depletion in the line power of this basic unit of police service. There are important alternatives to the conventional detective, particularly in the smaller departments with a personnel strength up to seventy-five or one hundred officers.

It is fundamental that tasks ordinarily assumed by specialized units and divisions that can be satisfactorily performed by the patrol force should be reserved for patrol so that its manpower may be increased and the strength of the special unit decreased. In cities and communities of 150,000 population and under, perhaps even higher, the presence of a detective unit would seem to be a waste of departmental resources. In such jurisdictions, there appears to be no sound reason for not locating total investigative responsibility in the patrol force.

As previously indicated, in those instances where the individual patrolman is in need of special investigative assistance or where the investigation might take him beyond the boundaries of his beat, experienced patrolmen, operating in plain clothes if necessary, should be able to perform this service effectively. Patrolmen can be selected for this assignment on the basis of demonstrated aptitudes and capabilities for the different types of case investigations.

In addition to the economy in money and manpower, this arrangement eliminates split-division responsibility for case investigation. In at least one known instance, this improvement has been made; there are undoubtedly others. The police department of Port Arthur, Texas, with a population of 66,676, has abolished the position of detective. The responsibility for all criminal case investigation has been assigned to the patrol force.

It has been indicated that the work of a patrol officer covers all of the major functions of a police organization, including the protection of life and property, the prevention and suppression of crime and vice, apprehension of criminal offenders, recovery of lost and stolen property, preservation of the public peace and order, and the regulation and control of traffic. On occasion, an officer does more than that.

A number of years ago, Michael E. Lillis, a patrol officer in the Police Department of Portland, Oregon, was transferred by his chief to what is known as the Albina section of the city. The Albina district was the star contributor to Portland's total crime bill. It boasted the highest delinquency and crime rates of any area in this city of a half-million people. Halloween night has been described as a reign of terror with juvenile gangs bent on destruction and looting. The forbidding fame of the Albina gangs who made the lives of police officers miserable was in full flower. Albina was a tough beat.

It was Officer Lillis who changed all that. He began by taming the once tough neighborhood. He started by winning the confidence of the youngsters. He fought for recreational and playground facilities. He organized all kinds of sports in the area and went after parks, swimming pools, gridirons, baseball fields and tennis courts.

He seldom, if ever, took a delinquent boy to court. He preferred to sit down with the young fellow and talk the matter out man to man. Lillis turned down opportunities for promotion in the department so that he could continue with his work. It was through the efforts of this officer that Albina eventually became a respectable neighborhood.

And so it was in the latter part of May, one year just before commencement day that the senior class of the high school in the area descended en masse upon the principal. They requested that the "Mayor of Albina," as Officer Lillis had come to be known, be permitted to sign each diploma in gold ink.

Officer Lillis answered the last call one afternoon while on duty at a school crossing. He had so many friends, little and big, rich and poor, and so many of them came to pay their last respects that the huge cathedral was scarcely large enough to hold them all. Some came in limousines driven by chauffeurs, some walked, some rode in busses that brought the youngsters from the Albina district. They remembered him for years as a police officer, and as a counselor and friend to young and old alike. The park in Albina is known today as Lillis Albina Park. He was the good policeman of the fiction writers, but he was real.

The Prevention Unit

In planning the organization of the prevention unit, it is necessary to consider its personnel strength. In a department with less than fifteen officers, specialization is generally to be avoided. Every officer must assume his proportionate share of responsibility for carrying out on his beat the crime prevention functions of the department. Where possible, the chief might assign to one officer the responsibility for coordinating the activities of the department in this respect. Again, the chief himself may assume this role.

In departments with a personnel strength of from fifteen to seventy-five officers, the need for specialization arises, with the creation of a prevention unit and the assignment of one or more officers to work exclusively with juveniles. Usually the assignment of 5 per cent of the personnel strength of the department is generally accepted.

Consideration should be given to the appointment of one or more policewomen. They would be especially helpful in processing cases involving girls and women, and boys twelve years of age and under. In the smaller organization on occasion, they can also be very useful to the department in many types of criminal investigation.

Functions

As pointed out by Kenney and Pursuit,* the functions of a prevention unit include the discovery of delinquents, potential delinquents and conditions promoting delinquency; the investigation of delinquency cases and the causes of delinquent behavior; the disposition or referral of cases; protecting the welfare of children and youth and community organization.

The departmental rules and regulations should clearly indicate the type of cases which come under the jurisdiction of the prevention unit. They usually include desertion, abandonment, neglect or abuse of children; contributing to or encouraging delinquent behavior on the part of minors; employment of minors in vocations or practices conducive to the development of delinquent behavior; bicycle theft; possession of pornographic pictures or literature; offenses committed on school grounds or in school buildings; sex offenses except forcible rape; and all other cases involving juveniles which do not come under the jurisdiction of other divisions or units, other than vice cases.

As indicated in the section on juvenile records, numbered offense reports must be maintained in the records division or unit, in addition to control case records in the prevention unit. Furthermore, the rules and regulations should clearly define the relative work position responsibilities of the individual beat patrolman and of personnel in the prevention unit.

THE OPERATION

An estimate can be placed upon the extent to which a police department measures up to its responsibilities in the approach to delinquency and crime prevention. In the rating instrument

---

*Kenney, John P., and Pursuit, Dan G., *Police Work with Juveniles and the Administration of Juvenile Justice*, 4th ed., Springfield, Thomas, 1970, p. 119.

that follows, each item is appraised on a graduated scale embracing five different levels of achievement, from zero to accepted professional practice—columns 0, 1, 2, 3, 4. The selection of the column in which the rating on a given item should be located is determined by application of the following evaluation criteria:

0—Problem not understood; see no need to be concerned about it; nothing being done.

1—Recognize the existence of a problem, but little or no appreciation of its significance; lack sufficient interest to take constructive action; management unfamiliar with the procedure or procedures required; no attempt being made to meet minimum professional standards.

2—Attempting to meet problem in a limited way; chief and commanding officers show some understanding of its nature and extent; substantial progress being made but still marked failure to meet professional standards.

3—Importance of problem recognized and fully understood; management active and moving intelligently toward solutions; professional standards being approached, but procedure requires further attention.

4—Problems approaching solution; established procedure now in agreement with accepted professional standards.

CRIME PREVENTION

1. Is the punitive philosophy still dominant in administrative policy?
2. Are limitations of enforcement appreciated?
3. Are minors detained in jail quarters?
4. Meaningful shift in emphasis from enforcement to prevention?
5. Administrative use of records data in the study of the nature and extent of juvenile delinquency?
6. Extent of operational planning based upon statistical studies and analyses?
7. Significance of delinquent as forerunner of adult offender understood?
8. Significance of the pre-delinquency period understood?
9. Repressive measures understood and applied in modification of the opportunity?
10. More than 5% of personnel strength assigned exclusively to preventive function?

11. Leadership characterizes the preventive role of police administration in the community?
12. Effective relationship established with Juvenile Court?
13. Effective relationship established with major social agencies?
14. Crime prevention unit operates within the framework of a social welfare point of view?
15. Active participation in community organization?
16. Systematic referral of acute cases for diagnosis and adjustment?
17. Effective follow-up routine?
18. Case-work approach to behavior problems encountered by the police?
19. Divisional in-service training for workers in crime prevention unit?
20. Local social workers, psychologists, and psychiatrists retained on training staff?
21. Personnel assigned to crime prevention unit university trained?
22. One or more full-time case-workers with degrees from reputable schools of social work?
23. Training in preventive techniques provided for all departmental personnel?
24. Close collaboration of police with probation officers in supplying Juvenile Court with case information?
25. Social, medical, psychological, and psychiatric implication of problem behavior understood?
26. Environmental risk factors and areas being attacked up to limits of community tolerance?
27. Significance of the police role in the pre-arrest period understood?
28. To what extent are the techniques of unofficial probation employed?
29. Patrol officers deal intelligently with emerging behavior situations?
30. Extent to which patrol force qualified by training and experience for preliminary contact with beginning behavior deviations?
31. Extent to which this training and experience are applied as routine procedure?
32. Systematic referral of persistent cases to crime prevention unit?
33. Crime prevention unit cooperates with other social agencies in bringing diagnostic and therapeutic facilities of community into play in individual case?
34. Invocation of arrest as a last resort is a principal feature of police policy?
35. Police administration and public school administration geared jointly to discovery diagnosis and treatment of the socially, physically, or mentally different youngster at the primary and elementary grade levels?
36. Administration has successfully reinterpreted police service to the community within a social welfare frame of reference?
37. Crime prevention unit under central control of commanding officer in charge of line operations?

38. Are all the resources of the community being utilized to the fullest extent in the treatment of the individual?
39. Has a community or coordinating council been organized in the community?
40. Do the police and the schools work together in all delinquency-related matters?

The elementary functions of a police department and its prevention unit include discovery of the case and its investigation. The strategic role of the patrol officer on his beat is here self-evident. Beyond this point, two general types of operations are observable in modern police practice. The distinction is determined largely by the procedural patterns employed in the disposition of juvenile cases.

In the first type of operation, the police function primarily as an agency of referral. Juvenile cases are referred to the juvenile court, to the welfare department, or to some other social welfare agency or agencies in the community and the disposition of the case rests with them. Wherever this type of operation prevails, the police have very largely abdicated their obligations and responsibilities in the project of delinquency prevention.

In a more professional and enlightened approach, the police prevention unit assumes responsibility for the disposition of a substantial number of juvenile offenders and beginning behavior deviation cases that come to the attention of the department and its personnel. In minor cases, the patrol officer on the beat may make constructive contacts with the youngster without referral to the prevention unit. Here, it will expedite records control if the name of the youngster and the action taken by the officer are placed on file with the unit.

In processing an individual case, the preliminary factual investigation is followed by diagnostic procedures, social, medical, psychological and psychiatric—in an attempt to identify those factors in the individual and his environment that have contributed to the end result. The clinical and social welfare resources of the community are brought into play in behalf of the youngster.

The circumstances may warrant placing the offender in the

detention home and referral of the case to the juvenile court. The factual investigation and diagnostic data, however, in the great majority of cases will not warrant such referral. Yet, *the youngster may require help in the solution of his problems if he is to escape later frustration and tragedy.*

Based upon the case diagnosis, the worker in the prevention unit assigned to the case proceeds to bring into contact with the needs of the youngster those procedures and those community resources which the diagnosis indicates will be of the greatest therapeutic value in bringing about a favorable adjustment. As in medicine, the unit of practice is the patient.

In the larger departments, the prevention unit should be staffed with trained social workers who are graduates of an accredited graduate school of social work and who are schooled in the application of casework skills and techniques. In the smaller departments where the caseload would justify the assignment of only one or two officers to this work, the chief himself or some officer in the department designated by him may assume this responsibility. He will find that there are ample resources in the community upon which he may call for assistance where this is indicated. These resources include the following:

1. Social welfare workers.
2. Consulting services obtainable from specialists in such fields as psychology, psychiatry, medicine, home economics, housing, legal aid and vocational guidance.
3. School counsellors and guidance workers.
4. Boy Scouts.
5. Girl Scouts.
6. Camp Fire Girls.
7. YMCA.
8. YWCA.
9. Boys clubs.
10. Catholic youth organizations.
11. Health department.
12. Welfare department.
13. Casework agencies.
14. Social welfare centers at universities and colleges in the area.
15. Civic organizations.
16. Churches.

17. Other character-building institutions and agencies.
18. Recreational workers.
19. Juvenile court workers.

Every police department, particularly in the smaller and medium-sized communities should make a complete written inventory of agencies, institutions, individuals and other resources in the area, together with the services they are prepared to contribute to the adjustment process, whether it be a youngster with problems in the pre-delinquency period or a confirmed delinquent.

In the early 1920's when Police Chief August Vollmer established in Berkeley, California, the first delinquency prevention division of its kind in the United States, he stated:

> The woman police officer in charge of the Delinquency Prevention Division, as well as each additional policewoman who may be appointed later, shall be a trained social worker, preferably with the stress laid on psychological and psychiatric training, as evidenced by a certificate from a recognized school of social work, or the equivalent of such certificate from a school of the first class, and she must have had some practical experience with executive responsibility in work with individual delinquents.
>
> The policewoman's work in Berkeley will consist largely in dealing with pre-delinquency problems. Primarily, it is intended to harmonize the agencies that are here in an effort to concentrate these forces that deal with the health, education and morals of the children upon the problem *long before he reaches the police station.*

There are those who disapprove of police participation in the treatment phase of delinquency prevention. Group work agencies have tended in some instances to resent what is referred to as an intrusion of the police into an area they consider their chosen field, and some judges disapprove of the exercise of quasi-judicial power by the police. The prevention unit is not an intruding and competing new welfare agency, but a police unit and a police philosophy with a social welfare point of view.

There is an element of treatment involved in every police contact prior to, as well as after the arrest, and it is a police responsibility to make these contacts constructive and beneficial rather than harmful. Regarding the exercise of quasi-judicial power, no police officer can be divested of discretionary power in determining the advisability or inadvisability of arrest.

Modern police practice recognizes the principle in dealing with juvenile problems that the arrest is to be invoked only

FIGURE 2. In every police contact with a youngster, there is an element of treatment; it can be constructive and can make a lasting impression that may linger on down through the years. (Reproduced through the courtesy of Bill Beall, *Washington Daily News,* Washington, D. C.)

as a last resort. It is obvious, therefore, that the discretionary power of the police in this respect cannot be safely undermined. In fact, it is in the prearrest period that the police are presented with the opportunity of playing their greatest role in the project of delinquency and crime prevention—in terms of the pre-delinquent. An unprecedented opportunity is afforded at this point for constructive police work. Intelligent attention on the part of the police directed toward the development of acceptable behavior patterns holds unlimited promise in making the ultimate arrest unnecessary.

There are those who take the position that the police are not qualified to undertake participation in the treatment or adjutment of delinquents and pre-delinquents. Admittedly, some police officers are not prepared or qualified for this type of work, but as Wilson points out, this merely serves to prove that they are not well qualified for general police service in the first place.*

Those who take some form of objection to police participation in the adjustment process occasionally make the observation that police headquarters is not a very desirable place for a youngster to visit or be taken. Two reasons for this view are usually given: first, it brings him into contact with the criminal element; and second, police headquarters, as such, carries a connotation that infers an unpleasant and possibly traumatic effect upon the youngster.

This is wholly unacceptable. In the first place, the only person who has the opportunity to see a criminal offender is a police officer; and in the second place, police headquarters design today presents an atmosphere that should make the youngster's visit to that installation a very pleasant and rewarding experience. Furthermore, elevated recruiting standards and the trend toward police training at the university level are making available a calibre of police personnel that gives the assurance of a constructive reception on the occasion of a

---

*Wilson, O. W., *Police Administration*, 2nd ed. New York, McGraw-Hill, 1963, p. 329.

youngster's visit to headquarters. Any police department that does not measure up to these standards should take steps forthwith to make the necessary changes and corrections.

In this connection, it has been previously noted that the universities and colleges of this country are now bringing their training resources into contact with the personnel requirements of the American police field. As of 1971, more than 350 institutions of higher learning were offering academic programs in preparation for career service in the police field. It can confidently be expected that within a comparatively few years, police training at the university level will blanket the nation, with a plurality of programs in each state. As indicated before, all this means that the potential and capability are there to ac-

FIGURE 3. New police headquarters building in Norfolk, Virginia. Police headquarters today presents a professional touch and an atmosphere that should make a youngster's visit to the installation a pleasant and rewarding experience. (Reproduced through the courtesy of Chief Harold Anderson of the Norfolk Police Department.)

commodate police interest in the treatment or adjustment process, and that this will be increasingly so in the months and years ahead.

It is relevant to indicate at this point that the number of workers in police service who subscribe to the philosophy of police participation in the treatment process is not overwhelming. Kenney and Pursuit, for example, in their notable work, *Police Work With Juveniles and the Administration of Juvenile Justice,* accept the practice of voluntary police supervision, under which the officer and the parent work together in assisting the child toward self-adjustment without the help of the juvenile court or the probation department or other agency. They express the view, however, that the police should not carry on a comprehensive treatment or adjustment program.*

This is a healthy situation for all concerned. Divergent opinions serve to stimulate inquiry, research, reevaluation and further refinements in practice as we move toward standards of procedure that merit the stamp of scientific sanction. Both sides can make important contributions. Meanwhile, the central point of importance is to see to it that by every means available, the clinical and social resources of the community are brought into contact with the youngster and his problems at an early stage when behavior patterns are taking form.

The conclusions of the President's Commission on Law Enforcement and the Administration of Justice are reproduced here because of their relevance to what has been said in the foregoing pages.†

All three parts of the criminal justice system—police, courts and corrections—have over the years developed special ways of dealing with children and young people. Many police departments have sought to develop specialists skilled in making the difficult decisions that must be made about the many young people with whom

---

*Kenney, John P., Pursuit, Dan G., *Police Work With Juveniles and the Administration of Juvenile Justice,* 4th ed. Springfield, Thomas, 1970, p. 124.

†President's Commission on Law Enforcement and Administration of Justice, *The Challenge of Crime in a Free Society,* Washington, U. S. Govt. Print. Office, 1967, p. 78.

the police come into contact. Officers have organized and partici-
pated in athletic and other programs to help improve police relations
with youth and enrich life in the community.

Correctional systems have established separate institutions for
juveniles and have emphasized probation over institutionalization
for juveniles more than they have for adults. The juvenile court,
even where it shares its judges with other tribunals or is not
physically distinct, has a philosophy markedly unlike those of the
adult criminal court.

Although its shortcomings are many and its results too often dis-
appointing, the juvenile justice system in many cities and communities is operated by people who are better educated and more highly
skilled, can call on more and better facilities and services, and has
more auxiliary agencies to which to refer its clientele than its adult

FIGURE 4. Another modern police headquarters building. Elevated recruiting standards and the trend toward police training at the university
level place the youngster in capable hands on the occasion of a visit to
headquarters. (Reproduced through the courtesy of Chief Jean R. Lane,
Maui County Police Department, Wailuku, Hawaii.)

counterpart. Yet the number of cases referred to juvenile courts continues to grow faster than the juvenile population, the recidivism rate continues to increase, and while there are no figures on how many delinquents graduate to become grownup criminals, it is clear that many do.

The Police Initial Contact

Whether or not a juvenile becomes involved in the juvenile justice system usually depends upon the outcome of an encounter with the police. Such encounters are frequent. Some of them grow out of a criminal act of significant proportions: the juveniles have been caught in the act, or are being sought, or there is reason to believe that they answer the description given by a complainant. In such instances, the contact is very likely to lead to further processing by the juvenile justice system.

On the other hand, many encounters are based on a relatively minor violation or not on a specific crime at all but on the police officer's sense that something is wrong. He may suspect that a crime has happened or is about to happen. Or he may believe the youngster's conduct is offensive, insolent, or in some other way improper. On such occasions, the officer has a relatively great range of choices.

He can pass by. He can stop for a few words of general banter. He can ask the juveniles for their names, where they live, where they are going. He can question them about what has been happening in the neighborhood. He can search them, order them to disperse or move on, check with the station for records and recent neighborhood offenses. He can send or take them home where he may warn their parents to keep them off the street. Suspicion, even perhaps without very specific grounds for it, may on occasion lead him to bring them in to the station for further questioning or checking.

In any given encounter, the officer's selection among alternatives may vary considerably among departments and among individual officers. It is governed to some extent by departmental policy and practice, either explicitly enunciated or tacitly understood. Such policies are difficult to evolve; indeed, in many instances they could not be specific enough to be helpful without being too rigid to accommodate the vast variety of street situations. Nevertheless, it is important that wherever possible, police forces formulate guidelines for their officers in their dealings with juveniles.

Besides the nature of the situation and departmental policy, however, police-juvenile encounters are shaped by other less tangible forces such as the character of the police force as a whole and the reaction and attitudes of individual officers.

The Commision recommends the following:

1. To the greatest feasible extent, police departments should formulate policy guidelines for dealing with juveniles.

2. All officers should be acquainted with the special characteristics of adolescents, particularly those of the social, racial, and other specific groups with which they are likely to come into contact.

3. Custody of a juvenile (both prolonged street stops and stationhouse visits) should be limited to instances where there is objective, specifiable ground for suspicion.

4. Every stop that includes a frisk or an interrogation of more than a few preliminary identifying questions should be recorded in a strictly confidential report for the record.

Pre-judicial Disposition

The Commission observes that it is a salient characteristic of the American criminal law system that substantial numbers of those who on the basis of the facts known to the authorities could be dealt with by the formal machinery of justice are in fact disposed of otherwise. The pressures and policies responsible for development of pre-judicial dispositions in the juvenile system are in part the same as those that have led to the use of alternatives to the adult criminal process.

Informal and discretionary pre-judicial dispositions already are a recognized part of the juvenile process to a far greater extent than in the criminal justice system generally. Thus, the informal and pre-judicial processes of adjustment compete in importance with the formal ones and account for a majority of juvenile dispositions. They include discretionary judgment of the police officer to ignore conduct or warn the child or refer him to other agencies; "station adjustment" by the police in which the child's release may be made conditional on his complying with designated limitations on his conduct; the planned diversion of alleged delinquents away from the court to resources within the school, clinic, or other community facilities by such groups as mental health, social and school guidance agencies; pre-judicial dispositions at the intake stage of the court process by probation officers or sometimes by judges exercising a broad screening function and selecting among alternatives that include outright dismissal, referral to another community agency for service, informal supervision by the probation staff, detention, and filing a petition for further court action. In many juvenile courts, the court intake process itself disposes of the majority of cases.

It is clear to the Commission that informal prejudicial handling is preferable to formal treatment in many cases and should be used more broadly. The possibilities for rehabilitation appear to be optimal where community-based resources are used on a mutual consent basis.

Pre-judicial Handling By the Police

The police should promptly determine which cases are suitable for pre-judicial disposition. The police should have written standards for release, for referral to nonjudicial sources, and for referral to the juvenile court. The standards should be sent to all agencies of delinquency control and should be reviewed and appraised jointly at periodic intervals. They should be made the basis for inservice training that would consider, besides the decision-making duties of the police, materials pertinent to increasing the understanding of juvenile behavior and making more effective use of nonjudicial community resources.

In cases where information on the child is needed, it should be obtained through home visits as well as from the central social service exchange and other official records. In addition to outright referral to nonjudicial agencies, the police should have the option to refer directly to the juvenile court specified classes of cases, including those of more serious offenders, repeated offenders for whom other and persistent redirecting efforts had failed, and certain parole and probation violators.

Police practices following custody thus should continue as at present but with two significant changes: Cases deemed suitable for adjustment would be referred to a youth-serving agency within the community, and the categories of cases that could be referred by the police directly to the juvenile court would be restricted. Exercise of discretion to release outright would be encouraged, as now, so that minor offenses not apparently symptomatic of serious behavior problems could be dismissed at the earliest stage of official handling, and even more serious offenses could be adjusted by referral to a youth-serving agency if, in the judgment of the police, there is no immediate threat to public safety.

There should be expanded use of community agencies for dealing with delinquent children nonjudicially and close to where they live. The use of locally sponsored or operated organizations heightens the community's awareness of the need for recreational, employment, tutoring, and other youth development services. Involvement of local residents brings greater appreciation of the complexity of the delinquents' problems, thereby promoting the sense of public responsibility that financial support of programs requires.

Referrals by the police, school officials, and others to such local community agencies should be on a voluntary basis. The agency's option of court referral should terminate when the family of the child and the community agency agree upon an appropriate disposition. If a departure from the agreed-upon course of conduct should thereafter occur, it should be the community agency that exercises the authority to refer the case to court.

It will be observed that the Commission's report treads softly and with some lack of relevance in the important matter of policy determination with respect to police participation in the treatment or adjustment process, as indicated in the section, "The Police Initial Contact."

The Commission further observes in this respect:

> Informal and discretionary prejudicial dispositions already are a recognized part of the juvenile process to a far greater extent than in the criminal justice system generally. Thus, the informal and pre-judicial processes of adjustment compete in importance with the formal ones and account for a majority of juvenile dispositions. They include discretionary judgment of the police officer to ignore conduct or warn the youngster or refer him to other agencies. "*Station adjustment*" by the police in which the child's release may be made conditional on his complying with designated limitations on his conduct may be invoked; the planned diversion of alleged delinquents away from the court to resources within the school, clinic, or other community facilities to such groups as mental health, social and school guidance agencies.

However, it will be noted that the Commission's primary emphasis is on a police appraisal of the problem and prompt referral of the case to a youth-serving agency or agencies in the community best prepared to serve the needs of the individual youngster. With this position, the police are not in general agreement. The report leaves untouched the potential promise of police participation in the treatment or adjustment process and police leadership in coordinating efforts of the various agencies and resources of the community into a program with unity and central purpose.

O. W. Wilson, former Dean of the School of Criminology at the University of California and later Superintendent of the Chicago Police Department, holds that there are four types of dispositions the police are in a position to make where a youngster has attracted police attention on the beat, or through the parents, through the schools, through the probation officer, or through a citizen's complaint—outright release with no further action indicated; police action in the treatment process through supervision on a voluntary basis agreed to by the parents, referred to by some departments as "unofficial probation"; a more extended treatment program supervised directly by the police and again on a voluntary basis, with the police bringing into contact with the youngster's problems one or more youth-serving agencies that are best prepared to serve his needs in terms of adjustment to an acceptable behavior pattern; and finally, as a last resort, referral to the juvenile court after all other measures have failed.*

Outright release of a youngster involved in some minor infraction is handled alone by the patrol officer on the beat, after discussing the matter with his parents. It is essential at this point that the officer file a report with a duplicate to the prevention unit, covering the incident, the circumstances and the offender.

Wilson recognizes the position of "adjustment officer" in the prevention unit and in the larger departments; he expresses a firm view that this officer or officers should be trained social workers skilled in the application of social case work techniques —including the disciplines of psychology and psychiatry—to behavior problem cases. It is plainly evident that he has in mind the equivalent of a child guidance clinic within the department,

---

*See Wilson, O. W., *Police Administration*, 2nd ed. New York, McGraw-Hill, 1963, pp. 321-353.

the extent of clinical services depending upon their availability out in the community. He holds, however, that the staff of the police prevention unit should be qualified to diagnose and treat the less serious cases of maladjustment without outside assistance.

Under the Wilson program, when the preliminary diagnosis shows little evidence of delinquent tendencies but indicates the youngster needs help in the approach to his problems, he is placed under voluntary police supervision with the consent of his parents. He is required to report to the adjustment officer in the police prevention unit for an indefinite period, the length depending upon the youngster's response to the treatment program developed following the diagnosis.*

Wilson refers to the third category of dispositions as the "adjustment case." This includes juvenile offenders who are not released outright, or who are not placed under voluntary supervision of the police, or who are not referred to the juvenile court. They are the more serious offenders who exhibit maladjustment to a degree that indicates the need for more intensive treatment. A thorough diagnosis is the first step in order to

---

*Minimum Standards for Voluntary Probation Program: Los Angeles Police Department, *Manual on Juvenile Procedure*, 1942, p. 15.

Time limit—No program of less than three or more than six months should be considered. Three months is the minimum time required to adjust the boy effectively, and in most instances the boy is just beginning to show marked improvement and an indication of satisfactorily completing the program by this time. In six months time, if the program has been conscientiously applied by the officer and absorbed by the boy, the case should be terminated as satisfactorily adjusted. Where it appears that a program of six months will be insufficient to effect the readjustment, the case should be handled in some other manner.

Agreement—There must be a complete agreement of the parent, child, and officer in every element of a specific program designed to effect the rehabilitation of the child.

Definite responsibility—The child must be capable and willing to shoulder the responsibilities entailed in following through to successful completion of the assignments of such a program.

Checking progress—A periodic check of the child's progress may be made through contacts in the home, through the school, through the regular office interviews, through sealed letters from the parents and delivered by the boy, and by a complete diary of daily occurrences kept by the boy. Many other means of checking his progress are available to the experienced officer.

identify those factors in the individual and his environment that have contributed to the maladjustment. On occasion, contacts with the youngster by the officer on the beat may turn the tide.

However, the diagnosis may indicate the need for the services of specialists in medicine, psychology, neurology and psychiatry. Additional sources of information in arriving at the dimensions of the treatment program that will be needed include the home, school and contacts with other social agencies such as welfare, recreation, church and the social service exchange.*

Once the needs have been determined, the central objective is to bring into play those youth-oriented services and resources in the community that are prepared to assist in correcting the maladjustment and encourage the individual to work harder toward developing into a successful young man. It is to be noted here that the police are not duplicating the services of any other agency; rather, the police function as a coordinating mechanism to bring these resources into focus on the problem. A secondary but equally important function of the police is to follow through relentlessly in order to see that the adjustment program in each case is being carried through by the agency or agencies involved in the case. In terms of records procedure, a case record should be made in the prevention unit on each adjustment case, in addition to the formal case or offense record on file in the records division or unit.

The final type of disposition recognized by Wilson is a last resort: the prior record of the youngster and the gravity of

---

*The increasing involvement of youth with drugs is cause for some concern. In the library of every department should be the following publications:

Bureau of Narcotic Enforcement, California Department of Justice, *The Narcotic Problem: A Brief Study*, 3rd ed. Sacramento, California, 1964. This publication presents in a forceful manner the more common types of narcotics and their effects.

San Fernando Valley Coordinating Councils, *Darkness on Your Doorstep*, Los Angeles, 19, 1969, distributed by the Los Angeles County Department of Community Services: contains important information that would be helpful to parents, civic organizations and others interested in the problem of juvenile use of narcotics, alcohol and glue sniffing.

the current offense for which he is in custody may indicate referral of the case to probation officers working out of the juvenile court for a determination of such action as they may deem advisable.

Legal Implications of Juvenile Court

Where the offense is serious enough and where the juvenile's prior record and other circumstances indicate referral directly to the juvenile court with the possibility of commitment to an institution, certain precautions must be observed.

In the first place, the case investigation should result in a preponderance of evidence showing guilt beyond a reasonable doubt, especially where the case is being referred on an allegation that the offense would be criminal if committed by an adult, or where there is the possibility of a transfer of the case to a criminal court.

In addition, there are certain investigational precautions to be taken. The Supreme Court in 1967 ruled on the Constitutional rights of children in juvenile courts for the first time in *Gault* v. *U.S.*, 387 U.S.° As a result of the decision in this case, it is recommended that investigating officers follow the same procedure prescribed by the Court in *Miranda* v. *Arizona*,† which held as follows:

1. At the outset, if a person in custody is to be subjected to interrogation, he must first be informed in clear and unequivocal terms that he has the right to remain silent.
2. The warning of the right to remain silent must be accompanied by the explanation that anything he says can and will be used against him in court.
3. An individual held for interrogation must be clearly informed that he has the right to consult with a lawyer and to have the lawyer beside him during the interrogation.
4. It is necessary to warn him not only that he has the right

---

°Gault (*In re* Gault 387 U. S. 1, 1967).

†Miranda v. Arizona, 284 U. S. 436, 86 S. Ct. 1602, 16 L. Ed. 694, 1966.

to consult with an attorney, but also that, if he is indigent, a lawyer will be appointed to represent him.*

In the smaller departments, with a personnel strength of from one to seventy-five officers, the caseload may not require such an ambitious program on the foregoing scale. Nevertheless, the overall formula set forth in the preceding pages can and should be applied, even if on a smaller scale. In most cases, the officer or officers assigned to the prevention unit will find available in the community or in the area, those youth-oriented services and agencies who are prepared to assist in the treatment or adjustment program, and even assist in the diagnosis. Only in this manner can a frontal attack be made on the problem, and only in this manner can the smaller departments of the nation make their proportional contribution to the total project of delinquency and crime prevention.

The foregoing concept and philosophy of delinquency prevention are based upon the early convictions of Chief August Vollmer of the Berkeley Police Department. They enjoy the support of Wilson;† they are subscribed to in the present volume and are subscribed to by the author in the first, second and third editions of *Police Organization and Management*.‡

Detention Facilities

Circumstances on occasion, such as pending adjudication of the case in court, may indicate the necessity of detaining a juvenile. *They should not be held in jail.* Where no appropriate detention facilities are available, a holdover facility can be

---

*See Dahl, Raymond A., and Boyle, Howard H., *Arrest, Search and Seizure* (Supplement), Milwaukee, Hammersmith-Kortney, 1967, p. 6. This work gives a suggested statement format to be signed by the suspect as proof that the pre-interrogation instructions of the Court have been carried out. Also see Penofsky, Daniel J., *Guidelines for Interrogation*, Rochester, Jurisprudence, 1967. This book is devoted to the obtaining and proving of a valid waiver of rights under the *Miranda* decision.

†Wilson, O. W., *Police Administration*, 2nd ed. New York, McGraw-Hill, 1963, pp. 321-353.

‡Leonard, V. A., *Police Organization and Management*, 3rd ed. Mineola, N. Y., Foundation Press, 1971, pp. 310-318.

prepared in a hospital or other fire-resistant building at a very nominal cost. In some jurisdictions, area juvenile detention quarters have been established. Plans for both local and area

FIGURE 5.   The appearance of the juvenile court is in deference to the philosophy that the child and the state have much in common and that the interests of both will be served by an intelligent effort toward helping the youngster with problems make a successful adjustment. First organized in Chicago and Denver in 1899, they were in response to the failure of institutional care. Today, the therapeutic emphasis has shifted even further upstream to contact the developing problem case in the early formative years of life when behavior patterns are just beginning to take form.

The increasing police shift toward delinquency and crime prevention has created new career opportunities for trained young men and women. Preparation for a professional career in this important area of police service should include a degree in police science and administration, with the collateral emphasis in sociology and psychology. In addition, the student should plan on from one to two years of study in an accredited graduate school of social work.

detention facilities can be obtained from the National Council on Delinquency and Crime (44 East 23rd Street, New York, N. Y. 10010).

COMMUNITY ORGANIZATION

All authorities in the field agree that a delinquency prevention program will move forward with best results if there is present some form of community organization such as a coordinating council, which brings together representatives from those organizations and agencies with a strong interest in youth welfare.

Such an organization should include the police and sheriff's departments, social casework agencies, health and welfare departments, the public schools, churches, civic organizations, patriotic and fraternal organizations, women's clubs, parent-teacher associations, representatives from such disciplines as medicine, psychology and psychiatry, juvenile probation officers, the Community Chest or its equivalent, and others interested in the welfare of youth. Obviously such a council functioning in an advisory capacity can do much in the general area of planning and in the fostering of a coordinated effort in bringing together the total resources of the community that would be useful in the prevention of delinquency.

The National Council on Crime and Delinquency,* formerly the National Probation and Parole Association, a nonprofit research and consulting organization, is the nation's leading agency in the development of delinquency and crime prevention programs. It has state councils in seventeen states and local citizens' committees in 135 cities. Regional offices are maintained in New York, Chicago, San Francisco and Austin.

The NCCD is especially interested in the promotion of community organization and invites inquiries from local persons and organizations, with the view of making their consulting services and counsel available. During the past half century it

---

*National Council on Crime and Delinquency, 44 East 23rd Street, New York, New York 10010.

has worked cooperatively with the U. S. Children's Bureau toward improving standards in judicial administration and correctional services and in the field of delinquency and crime prevention. The scope of its program and services is of direct interest to police personnel.

The following information is taken from the NCCD *Guide.*°

1. NCCD is a nonprofit, research and action organization that promotes and develops practical methods of crime prevention and control and advises on programs for the effective treatment of offenders.

2. NCCD is the only national voluntary agency in the country working with both the citizens and the professional in this field.

    a. NCCD's 60,000 members work with law enforcement, the courts, correctional agencies, social agencies, and citizen groups throughout the country.

    b. NCCD has state councils in seventeen states and local citizen committees in 135 cities. Regional offices are maintained in New York City, Chicago, San Francisco, and Austin.

    c. NCCD was founded in 1907 and incorporated as a national service agency in 1921.

    d. NCCD is supported by contributions from members, corporations, foundations, and local and state United Funds.

    e. NCCD is governed by a board of trustees, elected officers, and an executive committee—nationally prominent citizens serving without compensation.

NCCD aims are as follows:

1. To prevent crime and delinquency through early discovery and treatment of potential offenders.

2. To develop effective juvenile, family, and criminal courts.

3. To promote the rehabilitation of juvenile and adult offenders through appropriate correctional and community treatment procedures.

4. To protect the public from dangerous, violent, and incorrigible offenders by the development of programs which identify them and make sure of their confinement and treatment.

°*A Guide to the Services of the National Council on Crime and Delinquency,* 1968, NCCD. Also see *Standard Juvenile Court Act,* 6th ed. NCCD. *Guides for Juvenile Court Judges* and *Standard Family Court Act,* NCCD.

5. To educate the public on the nature and scope of organized crime—its costs and its consequences.

6. To stimulate citizens to act in their own behalf through community programs to reduce and prevent crime and delinquency.

7. To reduce the taxpayer's burden by eliminating ineffectual programs dealing with crime and delinquency.

Consultation and Surveys

NCCD provides states and local communities with expert consultation on crime and correctional problems. Services range from statewide surveys of courts and correctional systems to evaluation of city police-juvenile programs. In a typical year, field staff make at least 1,200 consultation visits, undertake sixteen major surveys, and complete twenty short-term studies on prevention and correctional facilities and programs. In addition, staff specialists offer consultation in the law, court services, penology, prevention, detention, probation, parole, community organization, and research.

Professional Guidance

Outstanding professionals in various fields serve as advisory resources to both NCCD staff and members. These experts include the following:

1. A council of judges—fifty of the nation's leading jurists, representing every level of the judiciary, including the U. S. Supreme Court.
2. A professional council—two hundred top correctional administrators, as well as leaders in education and research.
3. A council on parole—an advisory group of nationally known parole administrators.
4. A research council—an advisory group of leading researchers from the behavioral sciences.

Citizen Action Programs

NCCD sponsors state Citizen Action Programs which work with state and local officials to improve prevention and correctional services. Seventeen such programs have now been established. Backed by NCCD professional staff, citizen leaders in each CAP state (1) survey existing programs and facilities, (2) recommend effective and efficient methods of improvement, (3) inform all levels of the public about problems and solutions, and (4) act upon their findings.

NCCD sponsors voluntary local citizen committees. To date, 135 communities across the country have local citizen committees raising funds to support countrywide research, developing practical guides for police, courts, and correctional agencies, and stimulating citizen action programs, which involve the individual citizen in reducing crime and delinquency.

Personnel Services

SELECTION STANDARDS. NCCD publishes personnel standards covering education, experience, work loads, performance, salaries, and working conditions for professionals in the field.

TRAINING. Training workshops are an integral part of the annual National Institute on Crime and Delinquency, co-sponsored by NCCD. In addition, NCCD staff conducts workshops and training seminars on a regional, state, or local basis.

RECRUITMENT. NCCD is developing a recruitment program to attract young people of high caliber into the profession and the agency encourages colleges and universities to train young people for this field.

PLACEMENT. "Help Wanted" listings are a feature of the NCCD NEWS, a bimonthly publication of NCCD.

Information

NCCD LIBRARY. NCCD maintains the country's largest library on crime and delinquency. It is used by more than five thousand persons a year. Part of the collection is available for loan, and bibliographic and reference service is provided by mail or telephone, as well as in person.

NCCD INFORMATION CENTER ON CRIME AND DELINQUENCY. This automated storage and retrieval operation processes significant information from the United States and sixty other countries. The information Center's publications include a monthly abstract journal and listing of national project summaries, and a bimonthly bulletin, all going to experts in the field.

Publications

NCCD informs both the professional and the layman through a variety of books, periodicals, standard acts, pamphlets, brochures, professional journals such as "Crime and Delinquency," and newsletters such as "NCCD News." (A "Selected Reading List in Delinquency and Crime" is available from the Librarian, NCCD, 44 East 23 Street, New York, New York 10010.)

FEDERAL LEGISLATION

In the last ten years, the federal government has implemented its interest in the prevention and control of delinquency and crime through the enactment of legislation by Congress. This legislation has made funds available to states and communities in this general area of social welfare. Every law enforcement agency is presented with the opportunity of obtaining grants for underwriting the costs of appropriate programs. The foregoing legislation is summarized below:

Omnibus Crime Control and Safe Streets Act

Title I—Law Enforcement Assistance.
Part A—Law Enforcement Assistance Administration.
Part B—Planning Grants.
Part C—Action Grants.
Part D—Training, Education, and Research Grants.
Part E—Administrative Provisions.

Length of program and total authorization—Title I authorizes a five-year program [Sec. 512]. $100,111,000 is authorized for the first year of operation and $300,000,000 for the second year [Sec. 520].

Administration—Establishes a three-member Law Enforcement Assistance Administration to administer all grants. The Administration is placed in the Department of Justice under the general authority of the Attorney General [Sec. 101].

Bloc Grants—All planning grants and 85 per cent of action grants must be channeled through state planning agencies on a bloc grant basis [Sec. 202, 301 (b) 306]. Forty per cent of planning grants and 75 per cent of action grants to states must be made available by states to local units [Sec. 203 (c), 303 (2)]. Direct planning grants are available to local units if states fail to apply for planning grant in six months. Direct action grants are available to local units if state fails to file plan six months after receipt of planning grant. Review and comment by state governor is required on such applications by local units [Sec. 305].

Planning Grants—Authorized federal grants to pay up to 90 per cent of the cost of preparing a comprehensive law enforcement plan [Sec. 204]. $25,000,000 is authorized for planning grants for the first year of operation of the act [Sec. 520(a)], allocated in the amount of $100,000 for each state with remainder per relative populations of the state.

Action Grants—Authorizes grants to improve and strengthen all aspects of law enforcement. Purposes specifically mentioned are as follows: public protection, recruitment and training of personnel, public education, construction of facilities, control of riots and disorders, and community service officer programs [Sec. 301(b)]. In most cases action grants may be up to 60 per cent of the cost of the program but limit on construction is 50 per cent and higher limits apply to organized crime and riot control programs [Sec. 301(c)]. There is $50,000,000 authorized for action grants for the first year of operation of the act [Sec. 520(b)], allocated on basis of relative state populations.

Riot and Disorders Control—Included as a specific purpose of action grants [Sec. 301(b) (6)]. The administration is directed to give special emphasis to such grants [Sec. 307(a)]. Grants may be up to 75 per cent of the total cost of a particular program [Sec. 307(c)]. Up to $15,000,000 of the appropriation for action grants may be used for prevention, detection, and control of riots and disorders [Sec. 520(b) (3)]. Direct application for riot control grants is permitted until August 31, 1968, on project grant basis and without the previously approved comprehensive state plan.

Organized Crime—Included as a specific purpose of action grant [Sec. 301(b) (5)]. The administration is directed to give special emphasis to such grants [Sec. 307(a)]. Grants may be up to 75 per cent of the total cost of a particular program [Sec. 301(c)]. Up to $15,000,000 of the appropriation for action grants may be used for organized crime control programs [Sec. 520(b) (2)].

Salaries of Personnel—Up to one-third of any action grant may be used for the compensation of regular law enforcement personnel. However, such assistance must be on a 50 per cent matching basis with state or local funds applied to increase personnel compensation. The limitation does not apply to personnel in training programs [Sec. 301(d)].

Research—Establishes a National Institute of Law Enforcement and Criminal Justice to encourage research and development in law enforcement. The Institute is placed in the Department of Justice under the general authority of the Administration [Sec. 402(a)]. The Institute is authorized to conduct research, to establish a research center, and to make research grants to public agencies and private organizations [Sec. 402(b)]. Research grants may be up to 100 per cent of the cost of particular projects. Up to $10,000,000 is authorized for the Institute [Sec. 520(c)].

FBI—Authorized Federal Bureau of Investigation to establish training programs at FBI National Academy at Quantico. Also authorized FBI to conduct research and to assist in conducting regional and local training programs at the request of states and local governments [Sec. 404]. $5,111,000 is authorized for such programs [Sec. 520(c)].

Education—Authorized the Administration to establish programs of loans up to $1,800 per year and tuition aid up to $200 per quarter, $300 per semester, for law enforcement personnel in graduate or undergraduate programs at academic institutions. Loans are made forgiveable at the rate of 25 per cent per year [Sec. 406]. Up to $10,000,000 is authorized for such programs [Sec. 520(c)].

The following legislation was passed by Congress with the

view of strengthening the approach to delinquency and crime prevention.

Juvenile Delinquency Prevention and Control Act

1. *Comprehensive planning in prevention, treatment and control of juvenile delinquency and for strengthening of the juvenile justice system and law enforcement agencies.* Planning should result in the establishment of service priorities and program designs and should make provision for the involvement of available state and local facilities and involvement of youth.

2. *To assist communities in making available and promoting the use of diagnostic, treatment, rehabilitative, and preventive services to youth who are delinquent or in danger of becoming delinquent.* Encourages the development of innovative designs and methods of rehabilitation, improved diagnostic techniques and services to youth, intervention methods with respect to conflicts between youth and society, and the development of organization models and service delivery systems in the interests of juvenile justice. Also provides for the use of existing facilities (vocational education, crime prevention, job training, health, etc.) and coordination of services. Also encourages innovative designs and methods for prevention of delinquency including work with youth on probation or parole and establishment of services such as educational delinquency prevention programs in schools.

It further encourages the design and development of unusual and special purpose or innovative facilities for rehabilitation. Priority is given to alternatives to traditional probation, parole, and institutional care through residential or nonresidential services.

3. *Training of personnel in the field of delinquency prevention and development of projects for the training of personnel employed in or preparing for employment in the field of delinquency prevention and control.* This support includes the development of training materials with emphasis on understanding the processes causing delinquency, methods of prevention and control, and career related materials, short-term training for those working with delinquents or delinquency-prone youths, tuition for specialized training, and maximizing the utilization of recently developed techniques and knowledge related to the delinquency field for those already working with youth. Training priorities include training of careerists, development of

training capabilities of institutions, improving capacty of organzations to utilize training for internal staff developments, development of interdisciplinary approaches, development of curricula, counseling, and instruction for parents of delinquent youths.

4. *Support for technical assistance to state and local public and private organizations engaged in or preparing to engage in activities for which aid may be provided under the delinquency act.* In the form of information, data, staff, program evaluation, project planning, and feasibility studies to improve and strengthen programs related to juvenile delinquency.

Training—Grants may be made to any federal, state or local public or nonprofit agency or organization. Eligible applicants include, but are not limited to such agencies as state youth authorities, training schools, aftercare services, juvenile courts, police departments, colleges and universities.

Traineeships—For credit or noncredit training in approved colleges and universities—limited to one semester.

Chapter 5

COLLATERAL ELEMENTS OF THE PREVENTION PROGRAM

THE PERSONNEL FACTOR

IT IS PLAINLY evident that if the police are going to make a decisive effort in the field of delinquency prevention, the personnel resources must be present to make this effort possible. The specifications of the prevention program described in the previous chapter require a superior man in police uniform, superior recruiting standards, a superior training program and a salary structure that will attract this calibre of personnel. It is relevant to consider, therefore, some of the major components of a sound police personnel program.*

The personnel resources of a police department are its greatest asset, and this is particularly true in the area of delinquency prevention. All the way from the top to the bottom of the enterprise, the quality of personnel sets the stage for standards of performance in the delivery of police service. Furthermore, the degree of intelligence, zeal, determination and devotion to duty that a police officer brings to roll call as he prepares for his tour of duty is determined in advance by recruiting standards at the intake.

Fundamental to successful police service in the small and medium-sized community is the individual police officer, selected with care and well-trained for the job. The patrolman of today is the sergeant, the lieutenant, the captain, the chief of police of tomorrow. Thus, the character of police service for years to come is almost completely determined by personnel policy and very largely, at the intake, by recruiting standards. Police chiefs

---

*Leonard, V. A., *Police Personnel Administration*, Springfield, Thomas, 1970.

and other officials of local government are recognizing this basic principle, and as a result, recruiting standards are moving upward in order to bring into police service career-minded young men and women.

Entrance Standards for Police Service

Police entrance qualifications must be geared to the exacting demands of effective preventive work. Considering age, height, intelligence, educational background, robust physical and mental health, emotional stability and character above reproach, the man in uniform must be a high grade of human material.

In regard to the age requirement, there has been an observable trend toward a reduction in age limits. The police are realizing that the younger man is more flexible and more easy to mold to the aims, ideals and standards of the department. They learn easier and faster in the police training school. They possess more vigor, energy and alertness than the older men and are not likely to have their initiative stifled by some previous job failure. The career-minded man is the young man.

Today the age of twenty-one is widely considered as the absolute minimum limit for entry into police service. There is strong testimony for fixing the maximum age limit no higher than twenty-five, and there is strong evidence to indicate that men between the ages of twenty-one and twenty-five make the best material for policemen.

An examination of entrance qualification schedules in American police departments reveals a height range from 5 feet 5 inches to 6 feet 6 inches. The small man is invaluable at times in police service, but there is a psychological advantage that goes with the larger men in the control of people singly or in groups that is generally not overlooked. Most departments have arrived at the average of 5 feet 10 inches.

Where formerly two hundred pounds of brawn constituted the main requirement for service in a police uniform, the weight factor now possesses only a nominal significance. The requirement will vary from one jurisdiction to another, but most departments agree upon a minimum of 150 pounds. A reasonable and safe procedure is to consider weight in proportion to height.

The candidate for police service must possess robust physical health in every respect, as determined by a competent doctor of medicine. Equally important, reliable determinations must be made with respect to mental health, personality, nervous condition, temperament, social intellect, habits and ideals. The services of a psychiatrist in making these evaluations are usually available nearby.

The same considerations which dictate a rigid physical examination for all candidates suggest the necessity of annual physical examinations for all departmental personnel. From the standpoint of preventive medicine, incipient difficulties may be discovered and proper remedial measures taken at a time when they can produce the best results. Such examinations serve the interests of both the officer and the department, particularly in the small and medium-size communities.

It is extremely doubtful that there ever was a successful police officer who was not unusually intelligent. The highest degree of intelligence available is none too good for the trying tasks that daily confront a police officer. Rapid and accurate thinking is an essential quality of the police officer. He must reach decisions concerning the application of the law without delay. An officer's perceptive powers, his imagination, his ability to concentrate his attention upon the tasks that are before him, his memory—visual and auditory—and his reasoning and judgment must all be of the best. Otherwise, the individual must fail when confronted with some of the crucial tests that are the lot of every police officer.

Educational requirements in American police departments vary from the ability to read and write to high school graduation, with the trend definitely toward the requirement of a university degree in police science and administration. In terms of aptitudes, exceptional personal qualities are necessary for the satisfactory performance of police duty. Many of them are quite fundamental to successful performance so far as the preventive function is concerned.

The character and reputation of a police officer must be

unassailable. Police entrance examination procedure must include a state and national fingerprint clearance and a thorough background investigation. The application form filled in by the police candidate should be of such a nature that it will furnish a wide range of investigative leads.

One of the most disabling obstacles to career service in the police field is the "home talent" tradition still prevailing in too many American cities and communities. This expresses itself in the local residence requirement for appointment to the force. In order that patrol service in general and the preventive function in particular may have the highest calibre of personnel, the police and other officials of local government should take immediate steps to abolish the local residence requirement, in order to widen the field of selection. It is noteworthy that in recent years, an increasing number of communities have abandoned the residence qualification and require only that the candidate be a citizen of the United States.

The Search for Candidates

Following the establishment of adequate entrance standards, the next and perhaps the most essential phase of the whole recruitment process is an active search for candidates. Where the residence requirement has been disposed of, this can cover a comparatively wide area. Police departments and police associations in each state should take the initiative and pool their resources in the establishment of a coordinated statewide program of recruiting candidates. This would be especially helpful to the smaller departments, where the field of potential candidates is limited. In those states where state commissions on minimum selection and training standards have been established, the commission is in an excellent position to organize and administer a coordinated statewide recruiting program.

The Examination Process

Basic to the screening process is the written examination. The intelligent use of tests and examinations, now accepted as standard procedure in the best American police departments, will go far toward reducing the element of chance in the selection of police personnel. Contact with the personnel officer in nearby cities and the state police will prove fruitful in connection with the selection of tests and the content of the written examination. It should include at least one recognized intelligence test such as the Army Alpha, the Otis Self-Administering Test or the Henmon-Nelson Test of Mental Ability.

A probationary period of not less than one year, preferably two, is an indispensable feature of the examination process. During this period, superior officers may give close attention to the candidate's actual ability to do police work before tenure becomes absolute. No probationer should be given tenure until the end of the probationary period and only then upon the specific recommendation of his superiors. The department should be given the benefit of the doubt in all borderline cases.

Some form of rating system by which superior officers may at regular intervals appraise the desirable and undesirable qualities of the new recruit is a necessary and important phase of personnel management. Rating procedure thus becomes integrated with the probationary period as a continuing part of the screening process. Those individuals who cannot or do not measure up to departmental standards of performance need to be eliminated at as early a stage as possible. Effective rating forms, together with instructions for their use, would be obtainable from the personnel officer of police departments in nearby cities, or from the United States Civil Service Commission in Washington, D. C.

The Police Salary Structure

The calibre of police personnel carries with it important implications in terms of the police salary structure. In recent years, police salaries have moved generally upward. However, one of the difficulties in the past and in the present has been a widespread tendency to handcuff police salaries to salary levels prevailing in fire departments. This unfortunate combination is based upon the illusion that police and fire protection are of much the same nature. As a matter of fact, the day-to-day problems of the two departments have little in common. The police deal almost wholly with human relations while the work of the fireman is largely concerned with physical property.

All of the foregoing considerations pose important implications for the police in the smaller communities of the nation. Freeways, main arterials and other features of a modern highway system, together with the mobility of the criminal population today, mean simply that the exposure of the smaller community to criminal attack and other hazards has increased on a disturbing scale. The officials of local government would do well to reexamine their thinking in this respect with the view of adjusting police salaries upward to the point where they will be consistent with the quality and quantity of work to be done.

The Police Training Function

Even after police recruits are selected by the best methods available, the police structure will continue to remain unsound as long as it is generally assumed that a person with any type of training, or with none at all, is qualified to perform police duties.

Thus, an in-service training facility, staffed by the most competent officers available and operating continuously the year around, must be brought to the doorstep of every police officer in every department. Especially is this true in view of the fact that for some time to come, the police recruit must be accepted in the raw, unprepared for the rigorous and exacting responsibilities of police service.

Specific training in the techniques of delinquency and crime prevention should be made available to all officers in the department and especially those in the prevention unit. In those departments where an in-service training school is in operation, this subject area should be a standard part of the curriculum. In addition to using personnel in the department as instructors, guest lecturers from business and industry, criminologists and others at nearby educational institutions, social workers, recreation specialists, representatives from the correctional field, crime laboratory technicians, security officers, psychologists, psychiatrists and others can be brought in to reenforce the training program. Police departments will always find these people very cooperative.

In those departments where the staging of an in-service training school would seem to be impractical, officers should be sent to training academies in the area or to training schools in police departments in nearby cities.

For a number of years, the Delinquency Control Institute at the University of Southern California in Los Angeles has conducted an outstanding twelve weeks training program for police officers and others engaged in work with juveniles. Projected at the university level, its objective is to meet the educational and training needs of police juvenile officers and others in this field of interest. Classroom instruction is supplemented by field work and field visits to agencies and institutions involved in work with juveniles.

The Institute offers classroom instruction and seminars in four major subject areas:

1. *The causes of delinquency and crime,* emphasizing growth and change in childhood and adolescence and utilizing the contributions of the behavioral sciences.

2. *Delinquency prevention and control.* Here consideration is given to the police role in delinquency and crime prevention and other approaches to the problem, including the legal aspects, probation, parole and community forces, agencies and institutions.

3. *Police administration and techniques,* with a special emphasis upon the administration of police juvenile programs and the role of the law enforcement officer in today's changing society.

4. *Leadership and human relations,* stressing the skills of decision-making, problem-solving and communication.*

A police officer is fortunate indeed if he has the opportunity to attend this superb training program. The Institute has gradu-

---

*Kenney, John P., and Pursuit, Dan G., *Police Work With Juveniles and the Administration of Juvenile Justice,* 4th ed. Springfield, Thomas, 1970, p. 142.

ated in excess of 1,200 law enforcement officers engaged in juvenile work. A number of scholarships are offered by the Automobile Club of Southern California, the Sears-Roebuck Foundation, Hollywood Turf Club Associated Charities, Inc., and the Farmers Insurance Group. The American Legion Child Welfare Foundation, Inc., extends $300 living stipends to a limited number of qualified students. All inquiries should be addressed to the Director of the Delinquency Control Institute. Similar programs are in operation at an increasing number of universities, including the University of Minnesota, University of Wisconsin, Florida State University and the State University of New York.

The facilities are potentially available for an effective police in-service training program in this country and the police field itself is in general agreement concerning the curriculum content of an in-service training program. The problem is how to organize it and bring it into contact with those who need the training. The answers appear to be coming into focus and at an accelerated tempo during the past two decades. The American police services have now entered a new era in terms of their most vital resource—personnel. The time is now close at hand when the best in police practice and procedure will be brought to the doorstep of every police officer in the nation.

The new era finds expression on two major fronts: legislation at the state level prescribing minimum selection and training standards for entry into police service, and the emergence of police training at the university and college level. Both developments sharpen the focus on the American police field as a career service.

The New York State Legislature in 1959 enacted into law the Municipal Police Training Council Act, which led to the adoption of an 80-hour minimum basic training course, consisting of seventeen separate course subject areas. As of July 1, 1960, anyone appointed as a police officer in that state is required to satisfactorily complete the basic course as a condition for permanent employment.

The first year of operation saw the completion of thirty-five basic schools of instruction throughout the state and the award-ing of certificates to 822 police officers. It is significant that these 822 graduates are employed by 267 different municipalities within the state, indicating that the benefits of this police train-ing program have been broadly dispersed throughout every area of New York State.

Similar legislation was passed by the California State Legisla-ture on October 23, 1960, establishing minimum police training standards for California police officers and providing for the certification of schools where this training may be obtained.

Today in California, police training that meets the standards of the Training Commission is statewide; it blankets the state and exceeds by far any to be found elsewhere in the nation, with the exception of the State of New York. In California by 1966, 98 per cent of the population in that state was being served by police departments which adhered to the prescribed minimum standards for police training.

By August 1970, thirty-three states had enacted legislation establishing minimum standards for the selection and training of police officers. Of this number, in twenty-five states, the requirement for basic police training of all police officers was *mandatory.*

Apparently it is just a matter of time until every state in the nation will have established minimum standards for the selection and training of police officers. This means that police practice and procedure in the training of police personnel is on the way toward making total contact with the field, including especially the smaller police departments of this country.

As an important step in this direction, in 1966, a Model Police Minimum Selecting and Training Standards Council Act was drafted by the International Association of Chiefs of Police. It offers to the states a legislative model or pattern which can be followed in the establishment of minimum standards for the selection and training of police personnel.

Police departments and state police associations in those states where such enabling legislation has not yet been passed should make strong and effective contact with the members of their state legislatures and call their attention to these developments. Such action will accelerate the day when police personnel in all of the smaller police departments in the nation will have the benefit of adequate police selection and training facilities.

Today, universities and colleges in this country are bringing their resources for training and research into contact with the personnel needs of the American police field. It is now possible for a high school graduate to prepare for a career in police service in the same manner as the doctor, lawyer and engineer. As of 1971, more than 350 universities and colleges in the United States were offering degree academic programs in preparation for career service in the police field (see following table).

MID-1970 REVISION*
NUMBER OF LAW ENFORCEMENT DEGREE PROGRAMS AVAILABLE
IN THE UNITED STATES AND OUTLYING AREAS

	Associate Degree Programs (2-Year)	Baccalaureate Degree Programs (4-Year)	Master's Degree Programs	Doctorate Degree Programs	Number of Separate Institutions
Alabama	2	0	0	0	2
Alaska	2	0	0	0	2
Arizona	3	2	1	0	5
Arkansas	0	0	0	0	0
California	60	7	7	2	67
Colorado	4	1	0	0	4
Connecticut	7	2	1	0	7
Delaware	3	1	0	0	3
District of Columbia	2	1	0	0	2
Florida	14	1	1	1	14
Georgia	12	2	1	0	13
Hawaii	4	0	0	0	4
Idaho	3	1	0	0	3
Illinois	19	3	0	0	21
Indiana	1	2	2	0	3
Iowa	10	0	2	0	11

*International Association of Chiefs of Police. *The Police Chief*, Washington, August 1970, p. 68.

Kansas	5	0	0	0	5
Kentucky	1	2	0	0	2
Louisiana	1	1	0	0	1
Maine	0	0	0	0	0
Maryland	11	2	0	0	12
Massachusetts	4	1	0	0	4
Michigan	18	2	1	1	20
Minnesota	9	0	0	0	9
Mississippi	0	1	0	0	1
Missouri	5	2	0	0	7
Montana	1	0	0	0	1
Nebraska	1	1	0	0	1
Nevada	2	1	0	0	2
New Hampshire	1	0	0	0	1
New Jersey	13	0	0	0	13
New Mexico	1	1	0	0	1
New York	18	3	2	2	22
North Carolina	8	0	0	0	8
North Dakota	1	2	0	0	3
Ohio	11	3	0	0	13
Oklahoma	6	2	0	0	8
Oregon	10	2	0	0	12
Pennsylvania	14	2	0	0	15
Rhode Island	1	1	0	0	1
South Carolina	3	0	0	0	3
South Dakota	0	0	0	0	0
Tennessee	1	1	1	0	1
Texas	19	3	1	1	22
Utah	2	3	0	0	4
Vermont	0	0	0	0	0
Virginia	14	2	0	0	14
Washington	12	2	1	0	14
West Virginia	2	1	0	0	2
Wisconsin	6	1	0	0	7
Wyoming	1	1	0	0	1
Guam	1	0	0	0	1
Virgin Islands	1	0	0	0	1
	350	66	21	7	393

Recently, the International Association of Chiefs of Police, with the aid of a $400,000 grant from the Ford Foundation, threw the full weight of its power and prestige behind police training at the university level. It can be expected with complete certainty that within a comparatively few years, university police training will blanket the nation, with a plurality of programs in every state.

Indicative of the national recognition that is now being given to police training at the university and college level has been the appearance of incentive or premium compensation for academic achievement.

INCENTIVE OR PREMIUM PAY

In 1968, the police of Arlington County, Virginia, conducted a survey of some forty-eight police departments to determine police policy and practice with respect to premium pay recognition for educational achievement. The survey indicated that premium or incentive compensation was in effect in San Carlos, Gilroy, San Leandro, Ventura, Berkeley, Walnut Creek and Palo Alto (all in California); Montgomery County, Maryland; Wauwatosa and Madison in Wisconsin and Monroe, Louisiana.

Eleven, or 27.9 per cent, of the thirty-nine police departments responding to the questionnaire indicated that the premium pay concept was in effect. Projecting this percentage across the field in this general population class, it is evident that an imposing number of police departments have now adopted the policy of premium compensation for advanced educational achievement.

As a result of the survey, Arlington County adopted a premium pay program, effective July 1, 1968, giving a 2 per cent differential of the entrance police salary ($7,342) for each block of fifteen approved college credits (semester hours) up to a maximum of 23 per cent. The following table indicates the Arlington County premium pay scale for police officers:

ARLINGTON COUNTY PREMIUM PAY SCALE FOR POLICE OFFICERS

	A	B	C	D	E	F	G	G1L	G2L
H. S. Graduate	7342	7696	8091	8486	8902	9360	9818	10,026	10,234
One Year of College	7635	7989	8384	8779	9195	9653	10,111	10,319	10,527
Associate of Arts Degree	7929	8283	8678	9073	9489	9947	10,405	10,613	10,821
Bachelor's Degree	8663	9017	9412	9807	10,223	10,681	11,139	11,347	11,555
Master's Degree	9029	9383	9778	10,173	10,589	11,047	11,505	11,713	11,921

A new officer having a B.S. Degree would enter in "A" step at $8,663 per annum. After five years of service ("F" step) he would then receive $10,681 yearly. Should he obtain his Master's Degree during this period he would then jump to $11,047 ("F" step).

The above scale does not include all levels of premium pay; i.e., a new officer with 90 acceptable credits would enter at 12% differential or an "A" step of $8,222 annually.

Today, police recruiters are on the campuses of the nation seeking out candidates for the entrance examination. Many police departments now offer extra credit on the entrance examination where the candidate possesses a degree in the police science major. An increasing number of departments have established a minimum educational requirement of two years of college work in police science and administration. In some departments already, the candidate must present a Bachelor's degree in the police science major in order to gain admission to the entrance examination room.

The foregoing pages demonstrate that the personnel resources of police organization and management are moving into a new era of capability and performance, with all that this means in terms of the police role in delinquency and crime prevention. It all means simply that the potential and capability are there to accommodate the preventive function of the police and that this will be increasingly so in the months and years ahead.

Selection of Juvenile Officers

The rapidly growing emphasis on police training at the university and college level and the strengthening of police entrance standards is simplifying the process of selecting officers for assignment to juvenile work. In the selection process, the following criteria should be considered:

1. The officer's entrance examination score.
2. Educational background.
3. Field of study if the candidate has a college background.
4. Promotional examination scores.
5. Not less than five years line experience.
6. Service record.
7. Personnel record, including complaints and commendations.
8. Review of in-service training courses taken by the officer.
9. Evidence of interest in juvenile work.

JUVENILE RECORDS

The records system is the mainspring of a police organization. Its key importance in the planning and control of police operations is such that the author has written a separate book covering police records organization and management in the smaller department.*

Accurate and complete information must be available to the chief and his personnel concerning the nature, extent and distribution of delinquency in the community. The police must have the facts concerning the problem and this makes mandatory a police records system that will produce the facts, and equally important, it is also concerned with how to use them in bringing the power of the force into effective contact with this important phase of the police operation.

The Master Case Report

The basic element of the police records system is the master case report, referred to in some departments as the offense report or complaint report. The offense report is for the original entry of the facts concerning an offense or other incident that has been brought to the attention of the department. It serves as the first formal record of the offense and as the fundamental basis for headquarters' control over the case and its investigation.

But if records procedure should terminate at that point, the means for control over the case investigation would still be missing. The preparation of intelligent reports covering the investigation of a case is one of the major responsibilities of the investigating officer. Through the requirement that the officer promptly file a written report covering the results of his investigation, the means for control is established. The report is prepared by the officer assigned to the case.

Supplementary Investigation Reports

It follows that there may be two or more, even several supplementary investigation reports concerning a single offense pending final disposition of the case. Report writing is an art and one that is essential to the orderly and prompt conduct of police business. Some officers write more fluently than others, and for them, the

---

*Leonard, V. A., *The Police Records System*, Springfield, Thomas, 1970.

preparation of an investigation report presents no problem. Other officers find the writing of a report to be somewhat difficult at times. It can be said, however, that any officer, with some thought and practice, can develop a proficiency in the writing of a report that will convert the task into a pleasant experience.*

Follow-Up Reports

If the complaint or incident reported to the department for investigation is not fully disposed of as a result of the preliminary investigation and the submission by the officer of the preliminary report, he is required to make subsequent follow-up reports covering his continued investigation of the case.

The follow-up report is used by the investigating officer to report progress on the case, additional details, and any further action that has been taken. If the investigating officer has not submitted the reports as indicated above, the records unit should automatically, through its follow-up control system, note this failure and report the matter to the individual's commanding officer. The case should be kept open on an active basis until the necessary reports are submitted by the officer assigned to the case. Only in this manner can an effective control be maintained over the case and its investigation.

Prevention Unit Records

A copy of all offense reports involving boys up to eighteen years of age and all girls and women should be routed to the prevention unit, which maintains its own supplementary case files.† Other records maintained by the prevention unit include a separate case report or folder on each active or inactive adjustment case and an alphabetical index file on all juveniles contacted by the department. Where there is present in the com-

---

*See Hazelet, John C., *Police Report Writing;* Dienstein, William, *How to Write a Narrative Investigation Report;* and Gammage, Allen Z., *Basic Police Report Writing,* all published by Charles C Thomas, Springfield, Illinois. These books should be in every departmental library.

†Statutory age limit of a child may vary somewhat from state to state.

munity a central social service exchange, copies of these cards should be sent to this agency, as well as the schools and the juvenile court or its probation officer.

On all adjustment cases, the adjustment officer is required to file written reports at regular intervals covering his activities and progress on each case under his supervision. These are attached to or filed with the original adjustment case report. Copies of these follow-up adjustment reports are not routed to the central records unit, even though there may be an offense report on file in the case. The offense report should show as a matter of record that the case has been referred to the prevention unit.

Confidential Nature of Police Records

A tight control over access to police records must be maintained as a part of departmental policy. This is particularly true of records in the prevention unit. In too many instances, information that should have been kept confidential has been made available to unauthorized persons and organizations, resulting in unjustifiable embarrassment for a youngster. Control over access to police records has been something of a problem over the years in virtually every department. Federal agencies, including the Federal Bureau of Investigation, have demonstrated that the necessary control can be effectively maintained.

The problem is related somewhat to the whole question of headquarters security. Police buildings should be designed to circumvent unauthorized entry. Most police headquarters buildings are far from ideal in this respect. Areas within department buildings which are open to the public should be separated from areas which are designated for the exclusive use of departmental personnel. Public access must be limited to those areas in which police business with the public is normally conducted. Areas ordinarily used only by departmental personnel are to be considered restricted areas to which unauthorized public access is strictly prohibited.*

---

* Leonard, V. A., and More, Harry W., *Police Organization and Management,* 3rd ed. Mineola, N. Y., Foundation Press, 1971, p. 371.

Some authorities, including the U. S. Children's Bureau, recommend a policy of purging the juvenile files at regular intervals, thus implementing the philosophy of allowing young persons to approach adulthood with a clean record.* Opinions across the police field are not entirely in agreement with this recommendation. A study made by the International Association of Chiefs of Police in 1964 resulted in the following conclusions:†

> Factors to be considered in the evaluation of juvenile records in each individual case include the following:
> 1. The functional value of individual criminal histories in police investigations.
> 2. The research potential of the data contained in the records, bearing in mind that longitudinal studies of behavior may require information dating back many years.
> 3. The significance of the events recorded.
> 4. The fact that the skeleton notation appearing on a fingerprint record made in serious cases and forwarded to state and national repositories lacks explanatory and mitigating circumstances. Such a skeleton record may survive the destruction of the more complete data with consequent loss of explanatory material.
> 5. The feasibility of extracting useful statistical data and discarding the rest.
> 6. The fact that the record may ultimately prove to be a liability to the community in that it adversely affects the career of one who is truly no longer a behavioral risk, but a potentially productive citizen.

Based upon the foregoing, the IACP developed four important guidelines:

> 1. Police are, as a matter of policy, opposed to any blanket rule requiring the automatic and unconditional destruction of documents recording the police history of persons based on a criterion of age alone—either at the time they pass the statutory juvenile age or at age twenty-one.
> 2. Police should exercise discretion and judgment following the evaluation factors set out above and
>   a. Refrain from making permanent records of trivia.

---

*Kenney, John P., and Pursuit, Dan G., *Police Work With Juveniles and the Administration of Juvenile Justice*, 4th ed. Springfield, Thomas, 1970, p. 188.
†O'Connor, George W., and Watson, Nelson A., *Juvenile Delinquency and Youth Crime: The Police Role*, Washington, Int. Assoc. of Chiefs of Police, 1964, pp. 62-63.

      b. Periodically purge their files of records having no lasting value.

      c. Take steps through training and administrative regulations to insure that all records will be complete and clear.

      d. Establish tight administrative controls so that records will not be available to unauthorized persons.

      e. Provide explanations and interpretations as necessary when records are reviewed for official purposes.

3. Police should actively participate in deliberations, official and nonofficial, in which matters affecting police record-keeping policies are discussed.

4. Requests for information on juvenile records which come from other than governmental agencies should be referred to the juvenile court for reply. This practice will eliminate the problem of the police providing data lacking in final case dispositions.

FINGERPRINTING OF JUVENILES

It has previously been noted that in all categories of major crime—homicide, aggravated assault, rape, robbery, burglary, larceny and automobile theft—22 per cent of all arrests in 1969 were for persons under the age of fifteen and almost 50 per cent were under the age of eighteen.* When to this is added the circumstance that the human fingerprint is one of the most important investigative tools at the disposal of the police, policy with respect to the fingerprinting of juveniles becomes a question of major proportions.

The position is taken by the U. S. Children's Bureau that the fingerprints of juveniles should not be kept on file by police departments. Both the Children's Bureau and the National Council on Crime and Delinquency feel that no juvenile should be fingerprinted by the police without the consent of the juvenile court judge.

Wilson holds that as a general rule, juveniles should not be fingerprinted by the police because of the traumatic effect it may have on the youthful offender. He makes the point, however, that exceptions should be made in the case of the persistent offender or when the prints are necessary for comparison with

---

*Federal Bureau of Investigation, *Uniform Crime Reports*, Washington, U. S. Government Printing Office, 1969.

latents found at the scene of the crime. In this connection, the author recalls one police department where it was not only standard procedure to fingerprint juveniles but to take an extra set to be cut up, classified and filed in their single fingerprint system. As a result, the case clearance rate on burglaries was phenomenal.

The photographing or "mugging" of juveniles is not generally recommended; for one thing, the appearance changes rather markedly at this age in life. Secondly, photographs are somewhat limited in value for identification purposes.

The International Association of Chiefs of Police has appropriately found it expedient to draft the following set of guidelines in connection with these matters:

1. Any person, *regardless of age,* arrested in connection with a crime in which fingerprints have been found or in which fingerprints may be expected to be found on yet undiscovered evidence, should be fingerprinted for the purpose of verifying or disproving their personal contact with objects pertinent to the offense.

2. The contention that the process of fingerprinting is degrading or traumatic is without merit and the decision to take or not to take fingerprints should not be based solely on the age of the subject.

3. Where the police have reasonable cause to believe that the individual they hold is likely to repeat his offensive behavior in the future and that such behavior is likely to result in criminal offenses which generally have fingerprint evidence, the individual should be fingerprinted.

4. In cases involving habitual runaways, the police should fingerprint the subject for the purpose of providing a firm identification record for future comparisons.

5. The fingerprints of juveniles arrested for technical delinquencies rather than for traditional adult criminal conduct should be filed in "civilian" rather than "criminal" files since the purpose of such printing is solely to provide a reference for verifying identity as opposed to cases in which evidentiary comparisons are likely.

6. Fingerprint files have their greatest value in cases of persons who are recidivists. Frequently the ability to identify a recidivist depends entirely upon fingerprint records. Those persons whose backgrounds, environment, and attitudes suggest a high likelihod of repetitive criminal behavior should be fingerprinted.

7. The desirability of establishing standards and procedures for making certain identification records inactive or inaccessible de-

serves further deep study. Such study must be made by persons fully aware of all the factors. Thus, representatives of law enforcement, the courts, youth-serving agencies and others must be convened for this purpose. Neither the police nor the legislative bodies can act without full and complete understanding of all viewpoints.

CENTRAL JUVENILE INDEX

As a part of its general records facilities, the prevention unit will find it useful to maintain spot maps showing the location of juvenile offenses and the residence of juvenile offenders. The nature of the offense can be indicated by pins of different color or shape.

If a central county or area-wide juvenile index has not been established, no time should be lost in organizing this important records facility. As indicated by the International Association of Chiefs of Police:

> Police departments as well as other agencies which deal with delinquent youths should pool their information so that each may take action in individual cases upon the basis of a complete inventory of the youth's involvement with the law. Such central county or area indices may be established in any facility or agency provided there is 24-hour access for officers on the street. Such access through agency communication centers must be accompanied by swift and reliable interpretation of data by those operating the files.*

Only participating departments and agencies should have access to information on file in the central index.

The foregoing pages have been concerned with the nature and extent of delinquency and crime in this country and with the measures that society has taken in the approach to this major social problem. The primary emphasis has been on the preventive role of the police in neutralizing the desire to become involved as an offender during the early and formative years of life when behavior patterns are beginning to take form.

---

*O'Connor, George W., and Watson, Nelson A., *Juvenile Delinquency and Youth Crime: The Police Role, an Analysis of Philosophy and Opinion*, Washington, Int. Assoc. of Chiefs of Police, 1964, p. 64.

It is now appropriate to turn attention to deviation pressures and other factors in the environment which may exercise an influence upon the developing behavior pattern—all in terms of reducing the opportunity to become another statistic on the pages of delinquency and crime.

Chapter 6

REDUCING THE OPPORTUNITY

IN THE first place, it must be said that technological developments coupled with the professional growth of the police in
recent years have to be accepted as a strong psychological
factor in the youngster's mind in calculating the odds for apprehension. Two-way radio communication and motorization of
the force have almost synchronized the arrest with the
depredation.

PREVENTIVE ROLE OF THE PATROL FORCE

The prevention of delinquency and crime is a fundamental
role of the patrol force. The preventive role of the individual
patrolman on his beat is a basic element of modern police
service. The mere presence of a properly organized and efficiently operating patrol force is conceded to be one of the greatest crime deterrents thus far developed by organized society.

A basic responsibility of patrol service is the inspectional
function directed toward reducing the impact of police hazards
upon life in the community, particularly the youngsters. A police
hazard can be defined as any person, place, situation or thing
possessing a high potential for criminal attack or for the generation of any other type of problem creating a demand for police
service. They fall into the following categories:

Classification of Police Hazards

Persons

Criminals	Gamblers
Migrants	Drug peddlers
Alcoholics	Perverts
Drug addicts	Tavern keepers
Prostitutes	Pawnbrokers

Secondhand dealers
Feebleminded
Insane
Agitators
Fanatics
Subversives
Juvenile delinquents
Problem children
Solicitors
Peddlers
Car hops

Places

Main arteries
Streets
Roads
Alleys
Railroad depots
Bus terminals
Shipping docks
Warehouses
Taverns
Radical headquarters
Gambling places
Pool halls
Transitional areas
Foreign-born areas
Negro areas
Theaters
Dance halls
Low rent areas
Gas stations
Other business houses
Parks
School grounds

Property

Unoccupied dwellings

Fraternity, sorority houses and
    dormitories
Safes
Automobiles
Buildings under construction
Banks
Business places where—
    1. Insurance companies prohibit
       open stock risks.
    2. Open stock risks which are
       prohibited without alarm
       systems.
    3. Open stock risks which
       must be referred to the home
       office.

Situational

Athletic events
Political meetings
Parades
Conventions
Radical meetings
Unruly crowds
Demonstrations
Racial conflicts
Disaster
Mobs
Labor conflicts
Strikes
Note: police hazards must be fur-
ther classified as to whether they
are:
    High frquency
    Low frequency
    Seasonal
    Density
Temporary
Fixed
Removable

Where the police records system is properly organized and
functioning efficiently, it will always give a true picture of

police hazards in the community.* These hazards, with the delinquency and crime potential that they hold, demand continuous observation and attention on the part of the patrol officer.

In some instances, patrol officers have prepared beat spot maps showing the location of the various types of police hazards in their respective patrol areas, in order to insure that they receive appropriate attention during the officer's tour of duty. Different shapes and colors of pins can be used to indicate the class or type of hazard.

In this manner, a more systematic approach can be made in the observation of safes, suspicious characters, drug peddlers, taverns and other liquor establishments, parks, playgrounds, vacant premises, banks, theatres and other police hazards on the beat. Every effort should be made to modify or eliminate those conditions and circumstances which are conducive to the opportunity for delinquency and crime.

Routine preventive patrol includes the checking of doors and windows of all business establishments on the officer's beat and homes where the people are known to be away on vacation. In this connection, it is always good police work to encourage the residents of a community to notify the department when they are going to be away from home for any extended period of time, such as a vacation.

AUXILIARY POLICE UNITS

An important task in preventive patrol is the interrogation of persons on the street whose appearance and actions arouse the suspicions of the officer. In many communities throughout the country, the police have recognized the tactical advantage of a reserve force to supplement the observation power of the patrol force both in routine patrol and in emergency situations. In emergency situations, circumstances may arise where the available personnel strength of the department may not be entirely adequate to cope with the problem, and the avail-

---

*Leonard, V. A., *The Police Records System,* Springfield, Thomas, 1970.

ability of a well organized and trained reserve force may provide the difference between success and failure.*

Known generally as "auxiliary police units," these supplementary forces are recruited from among the responsible citizens in the community. Their duty assignments may involve routine patrol observation, traffic regulation and control along parade routes, at athletic events and other community functions, crowd control, assisting in surveillance operations, civil disturbance control, service under disaster conditions, road block operations, civil defense and other functions. In some instances, air squadron units, SCUBA diving units, boat flotillas and rescue squads have been organized as a part of auxiliary police activities.

It is necessary that auxiliary police units be recruited, organized and trained under the closest supervision by regular officers in the department who possess the necessary capabilities for this important assignment. Candidates for the auxiliary police unit should be screened and selected with the same precautions exercised in the selection of candidates for the regular position of patrolman in the department.

Opinion concerning the desirability of these reserve forces varies somewhat to a limited extent among police administrators. Chief Jacob A. Jessup of the Department of Public Safety in Sunnyvale, California, conducted a survey among a number of American police departments and concluded that the formation and use of a police reserve in Sunnyvale would not be in the best interest of the public and the police service.

Generally speaking, however, the police are finding these reserve units a very useful and functional addition to the regular personnel strength of the department. It is the general practice of members of the auxiliary police unit to serve without compensation. It has been found that the members of these units take a very special pride in their work and regard the assignment as one of the responsibilities of good citizenship.

---

*King, Everett M., *The Auxiliary Police Unit*, Springfield, Thomas, 1960. The reader will find this volume helpful in organizing, staffing, training, equipping and administering an auxiliary police unit.

A novel variation in the auxiliary police pattern or reserve force concept has been developed in Highland Park, Michigan. An unusual increase in juvenile crime prompted police officials in that community of 38,000 population to organize a Citizens' Night Patrol, consisting of five radio-equipped cars with from two to three men in each car.

On duty from 8:30 p.m. until midnight, they exercise no police power and engage in no police action of any kind whatsoever. Their function *is to "prowl," observe and report* any unusual or suspicious activity by radio to police headquarters, whereupon one or more of five uniformed patrolmen move in rapidly from their regular beats and take over the situation. Members of the Citizens' Patrol are unarmed and do not leave their cars under any circumstances.

Radio-equipped cars of other city departments which would otherwise be in the garage for the night are used on the Citizens' Patrol. The essence of the plan is that it doubles the observation power of the patrol force, and the officials of Highland Park have noted a sharp reduction in the number of incidents involving juveniles.

As another approach in amplifying the line power strength and observation power of the patrol services, the organization and use of the tactical unit or mobile task force has appeared in an increasing number of American police departments, both small and large. The tactical unit does not involve the use of personnel from outside the department. In order to consider the full implications of this type of reserve force, it is well to take a broad look at the total line operations of a police organization.

Operations constitute the field work of a police department. The line power of a police organization finds expression in two types of field operations. The first is "general operations," and these are concerned with meeting the normal daily problems associated with crime, vice, traffic and miscellaneous activities which are commonly referred to in police circles as general duties.

With trained men, properly distributed, the police chief can address the striking power of the organization in an orderly and effective manner to the routine problems associated with the general operations of the department—through the optimal distribution of the force by area and time. The degree of efficiency with which he achieves this end will determine in large measure the volume of special operations and the special assignment of manpower which this entails. However, even in the most efficiently organized police departments, occasions constantly arise requiring special operational plans and the execution of those plans.

Special operations are limited to the execution of temporary plans for the attack upon specific problems and emerging situations which arise at particular or irregular intervals. They are concerned with the execution of short-term plans designed to cope with situations of a temporary nature in order to permit an overwhelming concentration of police strength or striking power at a particular time and place, as indicated by the records.

In a small department, these emergency situations may develop only a few times during a month; their frequency increases with the increase in the size of a community. It is also influenced by the composition of the population and all the other factors which condition social organization. In the larger cities, these operational crises may follow in comparatively rapid succession and require almost continuous provision for the special deployment of manpower and equipment.

These special situations require an orderly diversion of the striking power of the department in sufficient amount to bring about liquidation of the problem. Therefore, there should exist and be available at all times a tactical unit or mobile task force representing the mobile power of the department which can be mobilized and concentrated in any quarter and at whatever hour or hours the circumstances dictate. The tactical unit is not to be regarded as a reserve force held at police headquarters waiting for something to happen, although headquarters may be its base of operations.

Members of the tactical unit are, under normal conditions, patrolling beats or carrying out the routine work of their regular positions in other units of the line, but subject to mobilization in short order for assignment on a special tactical operation. The objective is *saturation* in time and place, in accordance with data provided by the police records division or unit.

The operational pattern of the tactical unit is seldom the same on any two assignments and will depend entirely upon the nature and dimensions of the emergency problem or situation toward which its attention is directed at the moment. Police emergencies classify into two major categories, as follows:

Man-made	*Natural*
Criminal emergencies	Earthquake
Traffic emergencies	Conflagration
Vice emergencies	Flood
Jail emergencies	Tornado
Riot emergencies	Others
Demonstrations and mob situations	
Disorderly crowds	
Industrial disorders	
Prison outbreaks	
Others	

Criminal emergencies command the major share of the attention of the police in the conduct of special operations. Armed with the necessary data provided by the police records unit, police effort may be directed, for example, at residential burglaries in one section of the community, at car thefts in another, at armed robberies during certain hours of the day or night and at rooming-house burglaries at other times and places.

Thus, the striking power of a police department is amplified in this manner to a degree altogether impossible by the routine assignment of personnel. Members of the tactical unit should be selected on the basis of their personal qualities and performance record. The nature of the work may require moral courage, together with physical courage and endurance of a high order. The unit should be so organized and equipped that it can move rapidly from one point to another.

Through the reserve force concept, the observation power and striking power of the patrol force are temporarily increased to a point where it comes into decisive contact with police hazards and other factors, conditions and circumstances in the community which are conducive to delinquency and crime.

Aside from the preventive role of the patrol force, there is much more that can be done to reduce the opportunity to commit crime. In fact, as will be seen, the dimensions of the task and the challenge set it up as a *full-time job* for one or more officers, depending upon the size of the department. Since it involves every member of the community, it is primarily and must be a sustained educational drive under police leadership in which the opportunity is presented of making use of the wealth of communications media that are now available.

THE LIAISON OFFICER

Since the yield from the activities of this liaison officer is potentially very great, his qualifications should be carefully examined, so that the community and its youth will receive the greatest benefit from his efforts. He should possess an out-going personality and offer a pleasant appearance, as should every officer for that matter. The qualities of a salesman should be a part of his general makeup.

He should have behind him not less than five years line police experience and should be well adjusted in terms of his home and social life. A consuming interest and enthusiasm for the assignment and a recognition in depth of its possibilities should give him the drive that is called for. He should operate in uniform, with at least the rank of sergeant in order to give him more professional weight in his approach to members of the community. He should be a finished public speaker.

In the smaller departments, he could also function as the planning and research officer. Among his duties would be the development and refinement of the blueprints for the preventive role and activities of the individual patrolman on his beat. This could be a continuous assignment.

As a principal liaison officer between the department and the community, he would be instrumental in promoting the installation of burglary and hold-up alarm systems at high-hazard locations. This subject is important enough to merit more extended comment.

BURGLARY AND HOLD-UP ALARM SYSTEMS

In terms of reducing the opportunity for crime, the alarm system and its instaneous notification of the police is best understood within the frame of reference of the *operating time interval,* which is the elapsed time between the moment that a crime is committed (or about to be committed) until the arrival of an officer or officers at the scene. It can be divided into four well-defined and critical time periods, as indicated in the following diagram:*

$$\text{B} \qquad\qquad \text{C} \qquad\qquad \text{D}$$
$$\text{A}\underline{\qquad\qquad}:\underline{\qquad\qquad}:\underline{\qquad\qquad}:\underline{\qquad\qquad}\text{E}$$

The four divisions of the operating time interval, each with a specific function are as follows:

AB—the time elapsing between the moment that a crime is committed and the moment when some person lifts a telephone receiver to call the police.

BC—the time elapsing between the moment that the receiver is lifted and conversational contact at the police telephone switchboard.

CD—the time elapsing between the moment this conversation is initiated and a radio broadcast of the report to patrol cars.

DE—running time of the patrol car or cars from the point or location at which the broadcast is received to the scene of the crime or other incident.

At this point, the primary concern is with *AB—the time elapsing between the moment that a crime is committed and the moment that someone lifts a telephone receiver to call police headquarters.*

Because of the wide distribution of telephones in all communities, the telephone is the most convenient and direct means of communication contact between the citizen and the police. The time interval between the commission of a crime and the moment that a telephone receiver is lifted from the hook is an

---

*Leonard, V. A., *The Police Communications System,* Springfield, Thomas, 1970, pp. 16-25.

extremely significant one. It may vary from a few minutes to days or months. Some crimes are never reported to the police. Occasionally they receive almost instant notification, and on such occasions the law enforcement process has a reasonable opportunity to function effectively.

A reduction in this time interval may be made to a marked degree through well-directed educational effort on the part of the liaison officer. Through appropriate articles in the press, public speaking engagements, appearances on radio and television, and other communications media, the police are presented with effective opportunities to emphasize the importance of prompt telephone contact with headquarters following the commission of a crime, or—and this is equally important—the observation of suspicious persons, places or situations. Obviously, any reduction in *AB* yields a corresponding reduction in the total operating time interval.

Burglary and hold-up alarm systems wired directly to police headquarters hold a key position in the police communications system. In terms of the operating time interval, there is no lifting of a telephone receiver. Upon excitation of the alarm circuit, contact with the police is instantaneous. *AB* is reduced to zero as the apprehension process moves in to take the quarry.

It is interesting to note that in 1920, preparatory to its program of branch bank construction, the Federal Reserve Bank began a series of tests under the direction of Alexander B. Trowbridge, their consulting architect, in an effort to establish the relative resistance to attack of all known types of vault wall and lining construction and to rate these resistances in terms of cost.

Contractors were invited to submit their samples of vault walls and lining that met the most rigid specifications in terms of defense against criminal attack. In every case, *penetration was effected under time tests.* It is therefore a matter of record that the most modern bank vault, representing as it does the ultimate development in protective enclosures, is vulnerable to penetration by the safe-burglar, given the time and the tools. It is evident that burglar-resisting materials can never be more than burglar-delaying materials. If the burglar has time enough—and by that is meant no more than a few hours—and the tools, it is safe to say, that no commercially practicable construction is impregnable against him.

Nevertheless, whatever ingenuity can devise to delay the burglar must be applied. But the mere prolonging of the safecracker's task is not protection. This delay must be exploited to the end that completion of the offense is interrupted by apprehension. Therefore, a first prerequisite of burglary protection is an adequate alarm system which will deliver a signal to the principal source of help—the police. With an efficient alarm system, a pasteboard box can be made more nearly burglary proof than a modern bank vault not so protected.

Simply stated, an alarm system consists essentially of a mechanical or electrical device, usually a combination of both, which will automatically produce a warning signal at some specified point simultaneously with an unauthorized approach or entry to premises so protected. Through the alarm system, the request for assistance is automatically synchronized with the attack, and radio-equipped police cars may be concentrated in the vicinity almost before the perpetrators of the crime have had an opportunity to begin their work.

Because of its speed and silence of operation, the electrical circuit is the basis for all modern alarm protection systems. The simplest of all expedients designed to frustrate the burglar, that of contacting surfaces, is familiar to layman and expert alike. All devices in this category consist primarily of two electrical contacts, the disturbance of which will actuate the alarm circuit by one of two methods: the open circuit and the closed circuit.

The Open Circuit

In principle, the open circuit is exactly what the name implies. Normally, no current flows through the alarm circuit. Contact surfaces are attached at doors, windows, skylights and other strategic points in such manner that the unauthorized entry of an intruder will bring the two surfaces together, thus completing the electrical connection which closes the circuit and permits a flow of current to the terminal alarm signal. Although the open circuit is the most simple of all in design and construction, it has the serious disadvantage that the circuit wiring may be cut or otherwise tampered with, resulting in a complete paralysis of the system.

The Closed Circuit

In the design of alarm systems generally, the closed circuit possesses marked advantages over the open circuit. The alarm signal is thrown into operation by an opening of the circuit. Thus, any tampering with or cutting of alarm circuit wires results in an instantaneous signal at the alarm terminal.

Sound-sensitive Detectors

The perfection of the microphone made available a most effective instrument for burglary protection. These devices are extremely sensitive to sound waves of even low amplitude and are particularly applicable for protection against vault and safe attacks. Sound-sensitive detectors may be secreted at various places within the protected premises.

Although vault walls provide effective insulation against ordinary noise disturbances, these instruments are adjusted to pick up the slightest noise, and any attempt on the vault is promptly transmitted to the detectors, whether the attack is made by chiseling, drilling or explosion. This type of detector is so sensitive that it is set in operation by the sounds produced by burning tools, such as the acetylene torch and the electric arc. The slightest contact of the vault door, floor, ceiling or walls with hammer, drill, explosive or other tool is sufficient to operate the equipment and start the alarm on the way to its destination.

Heat-sensitive Detectors

These devices have been widely adopted in fire protection systems and they find a corresponding application in burglary alarm systems. A heat-sensitive detector is particularly useful when the burglar, in his attack upon a safe, vault or other enclosure, employs the oxyacetylene torch, oxygen pipe, electric arc, or other heat-generating accessories which are among the usual tools of the professional. It is installed inside a vault or other enclosure, where any fractional degree rise in the surrounding temperature is sufficient to throw the alarm circuit into play.

The Photoelectric Cell

This comparatively simple and reliable electrical device is playing an increasingly important role in the design and installation of modern alarm systems. It is adaptable to any standard current supply and any number of positions can be protected from one control point. In operation, this device is controlled by the illumination intensity of a beam of light falling upon its surface. A concentrated beam of light may, through the use of mirrors be made to travel back and forth over a predetermined area, and its interruption by any object will cause a change in the output current of the light-sensitive cell. This change in output current results in the operation of the signal circuit proper. It is thus possible to blanket a protected interior with a screen of light of any desired shape. Penetration of the light wall by any object puts the alarm circuit into play.

Radio Frequency Circuits

The radio frequency circuit is designed to detect and report the approach of an object through the amplification of changes in the inductive and capacitive characteristics of the surrounding air. Application of the radio frequency circuit to alarm installations is based upon the fact that if an object is brought near an oscillating circuit which is not shielded, changes occur in the tuning of the circuit. These changes cause very definite variations in the current characteristics of the circuit, which may be easily amplified and used to move the necessary relay apparatus and get the alarm signal on its way.

It is thus evident that in the design of burglary alarm systems, no problems of any importance are presented. In respect to the crime of robbery, however, the design of the exciting mechanism is more complicated because of the inherent characteristics of the crime. Robbery is an offense against both person and property. It has all the esential elements of larceny, with the additional requirement that the property must be taken from the person of the victim, and against his will, by means of force or fear. It is essential in robbery that the criminal offender approach the victim personally and by means of force or fear complete the crime.

The average time required to complete a bank robbery may be less than two minutes; a burglary may be a matter of a few minutes or an entire weekend. A study of 150 bank robberies in Los Angeles revealed that in most instances, the offense was completed in less than three minutes. Where the burglar may encounter any number of physical barriers in effecting entry, the daylight bandit walks through an open door the same as any customer.

The problem of placing the robbery alarm circuit in operation is therefore more involved than is the case in a burglary alarm system installation. In many hold-up alarm installations, the "touch-off" is accomplished by means of contact devices such as push buttons and footrails placed at convenient points in the bank interior. There are many variations of this device, but they all require manual push button or pedal operation, usually by the victim.

This method of originating the alarm signal, although better than no protection at all, is open to serious criticism, since the victim may have to risk his or her life in order to send in the alarm. There is an approach to the problem, however, which appears to hold considerable promise.

Since the object of attack in bank robbery is invariably currency, alarm circuit exciting devices may be built into specially designed currency trays, drawers or other containers where money is normally kept. A false bottom, for example, may be so arranged so that when the command, "put it in the bag," comes, a slight pressure downward when removing the bills will excite the alarm circuit.*

---

*A bank in Fort Worth, Texas, has designed and put into operation a drive-in banking unit with six tellers who are entirely unexposed so far as a potential holdup is concerned; they communicate with the individual outside in his car via a television screen.

The police in small and medium-sized cities and communities should lose no time in gaining the cooperation of banks, jewelry stores, theaters and other high-hazard locations, in arranging for the design and installation of appropriate alarm systems wired directly to police headquarters. Alarm circuit installations present no serious problem. Through consultation by the liaison officer with the officials of the local telephone company and the city electrician, the answers will be forthcoming. The increase in apprehension capability which the alarm circuit gives, places it high on the agenda of the police and the establishments in the community which need this protection.*

In addition to the foregoing, the American District Telegraph Company, whose primary business is alarm systems, installs, operates and maintains alarm systems covering fire, burglary and hold-up. Alarm system terminals are wired directly to their own control stations, from which they dispatch their own personnel in the emergency after notifying the police. Honeywell Security Systems also operates a similar service. Furthermore, the smaller department usually has convenient access to nearby cities in which will be found a number of other commercial concerns who specialize in alarm systems counseling and their installation.

Burglary, hold-up and fire alarm systems have a high investment yield in terms of reducing the opportunity and increasing the certainty of apprehension. Few burglars, hold-up men and arsonists will attack a premises known to be protected with an alarm system. An increasing number of banks have installed concealed motion picture cameras which make a photographic

---

*Important sources of security information concerning alarm circuit engineering include the following—Alarmtronics Engineering, Inc., 154 California Street, Newton, Massachusetts 02195; American District Telegraph Co., 155 Sixth Avenue, New York, N. Y., 10013; Babaco Alarm System, Inc., 202 Park Street, Miami Springs, Florida 33166; Mosler Safe Company, 1561 Grand Blvd., Hamilton, Ohio 45011; and Pyrontronics, Inc., 2343 Morris Avenue, Union, New Jersey.

Also see Post, Richard S., and Kingsbury, Arthur A., *Security Administration*, Springfield, Thomas, 1970.

record of the event in case of bank robbery. More than one stick-up man has made his way to the penitentiary because his face and general appearance were photographed for the record.

The President's Commission on Law Enforcement and Administration of Justice has this to say in regard to reducing the opportunity to commit crime:°

> There are a number of immediate ways in which technology can address itself to specific problems in crime prevention. Technology is directly applicable to reducing criminal opportunities through protecting or "hardening" targets of crime, by making them less vulnerable to theft and by inhibiting criminal activity. Homes and valuables can be protected by better safes and locks; magnetic inks can be used to curtail the use of bogus checks; photographs on credit cards would reduce their improper use; eventually, store owners will be able to establish immediate identity and sufficiency of credit rating with the aid of electronic data processing.

Hardening the Target in Auto Theft

The automobile is a common target of theft which is particularly susceptible to hardening devices. It accounts for about one-third of Part I crimes in the United States. Auto theft, larceny of auto accessories and larceny from autos each represent about 11 per cent of Part I crimes. Design changes in automobiles making accessories such as hub caps, seats, radios and batteries less easily removed could reduce the illegal traffic in these items.

Increasing the Difficulty of Auto Theft

Auto theft is prevalent and costly. The Commission reported that in 1965, 486,000 autos valued at over 500 million dollars were stolen. About 28 per cent of the inhabitants of federal prisons are there as a result of conviction of interstate auto theft under the Dyer Act. In California alone, auto thefts cost the criminal justice system over 60 million dollars annually.

°President's Commission on Law Enforcement and Administration of Justice, *Task Force Report Science and Technology*, Washington, U. S. Gov. Print. Office, 1970, p. 48.

The great majority of auto thefts is for temporary use rather than resale, as evidenced by the fact that 88 per cent of autos stolen in 1965 were recovered. In Los Angeles, 64 per cent of autos that were recovered were found within two days and about 80 per cent within a week. Chicago reports that 71 per cent of the recovered autos were found within four miles of the point of theft. Data from Berkeley showed that 82 per cent of recovered autos were found in Berkeley or in police jurisdictions contiguous to it. The Federal Bureau of Investigation estimates that 8 per cent of stolen cars are taken for the purpose of stripping them for parts, 12 per cent for resale, and 5 per cent for use in another crime.

Auto thefts are primarily juvenile acts. Although only 21 per cent of all arrests for nontraffic offenses in 1965 were of individuals under eighteen years of age, 63 per cent of auto theft arrests were of persons under eighteen years of age. Auto theft marks the beginning of many criminal careers; in an FBI sample of juvenile auto theft offenders, 41 per cent had no prior arrest record.

The theft may come about simply because a boy sees an unlocked automobile readily available, not infrequently with the ignition key in the switch. Berkeley reported that 49 per cent of the autos stolen in 1965 had a key left in the ignition or the ignition open. Milwaukee reports that 37 per cent of the autos stolen had the ignition open or a key in the switch. The FBI observes that, nationwide, 42 per cent of the autos stolen had the key in the ignition or the ignition unlocked. Even of those taken when the keys were out, at least 20 per cent are stolen by merely shorting the ignition circuit with tools as simple as jumper wires, paper clips, tinfoil and coins.

The effects of changing the ignition system to make auto theft more difficult were studied on the basis of the St. Louis experience. Chart XII shows by make and model year the number of cars reported stolen in St. Louis in the first eight months of 1966. The Chevrolet was the most frequently stolen car, well out of proportion to its registration for models prior to 1965. Chart XII also shows the ratio of these numbers of stolen cars to Missouri

CHART XII

Auto Thefts as a Function of Make and Model Year

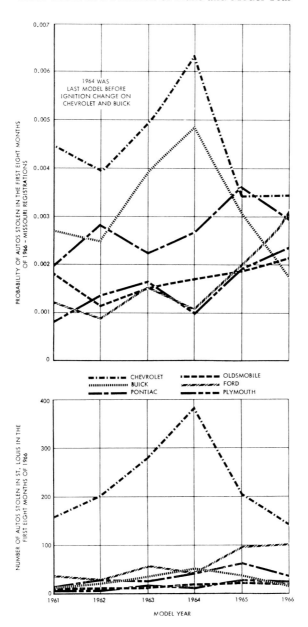

registration totals, i.e., the probability, by make and model of car registered in Missouri having been stolen in 1966.

The sharp drop in theft probabilities of the 1965 and 1966 models indicates that the change in the Chevrolet lock (eliminating the unlocked "off" position in 1965 resulted in about 50 per cent fewer 1965 Chevrolets stolen than the previous year's models. A similar effect occurred for Buick theft probabilities, due to a similar ignition change. The increase in theft of the other makes was overshadowed by the decrease in Chevrolet and Buick thefts. Thus, the 1965 Chevrolet and Buick owners in that year and after had more protection than the owners of previous years' models.

These findings suggest that the easy opportunity to take a car may contribute significantly to auto theft and that thefts by the relatively casual or marginal offender would be reduced by making theft more difficult than merely starting the car. Educational campaigns advising drivers to remove their ignitions keys and to lock their cars are important. Some cities have ordinances imposing penalties on drivers who leave keys in unattended vehicles. Lock design has been aimed at increasing the number of different key combinations in order to reduce auto thefts due to "try-out" or "master" keys.

A more fundamental change in the ignition system and other automobile components is needed. Many possibilities exist. Spring ejection locks can prevent the driver from leaving the key in the ignition; sturdier housings can enclose ignition terminals; heavier metal cable can surround the ignition wires; steering-wheel or transmission-locking devices can be used, as is done on several foreign cars.

The problem has been discussed by Task Force and Department of Justice representatives with the four major automobile manufacturers. The manufacturers have agreed to develop and install devices to increase the security of their products. These will include making the ignition system connector cable much more difficult to remove from the ignition lock, increasing the ignition key combinations, and locating the ignition system in less accessible places. These basic improvements were to be made in the 1968 models. One manufacturer installed on its 1968 models a buzzer which signals the driver when he opens the door that he has left his key in the ignition lock.

Although the above steps will contribute to reducing the opportunity for automobile theft, the following additional improvements should be carefully considered:

> A steering column and/or transmission lock which immobilizes the car when the gear-shift lever is put into the proper position and the key removed. With this type of lock, starting an engine by shorting the ignition does not permit the car to be driven away. An ignition system which causes the driver to remove the key from the ignition is recommended. This can be done by a spring-loaded lock or key which pushes the key out; or by requiring the key to be not only turned but also pulled out of the ignition in order to stop the engine; or by attaching a buzzer which goes off if the key is left in the ignition when the engine is turned off.

Although the automobile manufacturers are best able to integrate such devices into the design of their vehicles, it is desirable that some federal agency work with them to establish minimum requirements on the actual implementation. This responsibility could well be assigned to the National Highway Safety Bureau as part of its program to establish safety standards for automobiles.

STREET LIGHTING

The evidence indicates the probability of a strong correlation between candlepower and the burglary rate as well as the rate on other crimes. The President's Commission observes:

"Improved street lighting is frequently advocated by the police and highway departments as an important tool for reducing the opportunity to commit crime. Its proponents believe that adequate street lighting will (1) deter certain types of street crimes by increasing the risk of detection of the offender; and (2) enhance the probability of apprehending the offender. These assumptions are fortified by the general sense of security which is induced in the individual by the presence of adequate street lighting."

Since much of crime occurs at night, there is considerable intuitive support for the feeling that street lighting will suppress the incidence of crime. According to data compiled by the Los Angeles Police Department during the year 1965, there were 164,000 reported offenses and attempts. Of these 49,000 were committed during the day, 75,000 at night, and 40,000 at unknown times. Likewise, certain crimes such as robbery, aggravated assault, purse snatching and rape, have a higher probability of being perpetrated at night.

In 1956, the central business district of Flint, Michigan, was relighted. Six-thousand-lumen incandescent lights were replaced with 20,000-lumen multiple fluorescent bracket-type lights. A study over a six-month period indicated that there was a 60 per cent reduction in the number of felonies and misdemeanors, and 80 per cent reduction in the number of larcenies. However, there was, at the same time, an increase in police surveillance in the area. Since the experiment was not controlled, the effects of patrol and relighting are combined, so that any conclusions on the effects of street lighting must be considered only tentative.

In New York City, four police precincts designated as high crime areas were converted from incandescent lighting to mercury vapor lighting. The rate of nighttime crimes dropped by 49 per cent after the installation of the lights. In 1964, after 80 per cent of the city street lighting had been converted over a four-year period at a cost of 58 million dollars, the total felonies in the city increased by approximately 43 per cent. It is impossible to determine what the felony rate would have been if the lights had not been installed.

In St. Louis, there seems to exist evidence of a favorable impact by street lighting on certain types of crime. A program of improved street lighting was first begun in 1964 in a principal business district in the downtown area. In a comparison of recorded criminal acts in 1963 with those of 1965, it was found that crimes against the person decreased by 40.8 per cent, auto theft by 28.6 per cent, and business burglaries by 12.8 per cent. In another study involving a high crime district known as Central West End, an increase in crimes was recorded, but the rate of increase was not as high as in the surrounding areas. In addition, the overall increase of crime was lower than anticipated in these two areas.

At present, the only conclusions it is possible to reach now are as follows:

1. There is no conclusive evidence that improved lighting will have lasting or significant impact on crime rates, although there are strong intuitive reasons to believe that it will be helpful.
2. Improved street lighting may reduce some types of crimes in some areas, i.e., given a light and dark street to commit a crime, a criminal offender will probably choose the dark street.
3. Improved street lighting accompanied by increased police patrol can reduce the opportunity to commit crime in an area.
4. When new lighting programs are instituted, police departments should be encouraged to maintain records of crimes in the relighted and adjoining areas. With information on past, present and projected crime rates, it may be possible to assess better the impact of lighting on crime.

It is agreed that some objective research is indicated in order to establish on a more scientific basis the correlation between candlepower and the opportunity to commit crime. It is the opinion of the author, however, that the President's Commission could justifiably have given the need for better street lighting a more affirmative support than "intuitive reasons to believe that it would be helpful."

The police are convinced. Their warning to women, for example, when out at night to confine their movement to well-illuminated areas, speaks for itself. Thus, with no room for doubt, the police in every community should exert their best effort in gaining the interest and support of the officials of local government in the installation of acceptable street lighting.

GAINING COMMUNITY COOPERATION

The police are in a prime position to energize the interest and support of members of the community in taking effective steps to reduce the opportunity to become involved in delinquency and crime. In this respect, the President's Commission stated,* "Public education to alert citizens and businessmen on how to avoid becoming victims of crime can be a valuable adjunct to a crime control program. In many instances, such campaigns are undertaken by the police. In other cases they are sponsored by interested citizens, civic organizations and businessmen's groups. The best ones are often the result of a cooperative effort."

The American Association of Federated Women's Clubs and the National Auto Theft Bureau have conducted auto theft prevention campaigns in several cities, accompanying the police on their rounds, leaving pamphlets in unlocked cars and attaching warnings to parking meters on the dangers of leaving keys in the ignition switch.

Another women's organization, the General Federation of Women's Clubs, has campaigned for better street lighting throughout the country. Businesses ranging from grocery chains to banks and diaper institutes have paid for pamphlets distributed to their customers on precautionary measures citizens may take to avoid becoming the victims of crime. The Insurance Institute has made special appeals to clients on safeguarding furs and jewelry. The service clubs in one city bought etching tools so that the police could imprint serial numbers on valuable possessions of willing citizens. In another community, similar groups have provided a film library so that the local police department could supplement their appearances before citizens and school groups with moving pictures on such subjects as vandalism, narcotics, personal defense, and burglary protection. A mid-western sheriff has a "junior posse" of over 25,000 youngsters who distribute crime prevention literature to homeowners and apartment residents.

The police of several European countries, including Finland, Germany and Sweden, are engaged in special programs which could be utilized by American police forces. They have police

---

*President's Commission on Law Enforcement and Administration of Justice, *Task Force Report: The Police*, Washington, U. S. Gov. Print. Office, 1970, p. 222

advisory storefront offices set up in the cities and staffed by police officers ready to offer advice to citizens. An English Home Office report has considered cataloging in central registries the crime prevention exhibits of local police forces to permit interchange of exhibits and successful techniques. The report also describes the experience of the English police with the crime prevention officer who is especially detailed to call on victims, offer advice and follow-up services, distribute crime prevention literature, undertake security needs studies and train police force members in prevention techniques.

In 1967, under a grant by the Office of Law Enforcement Assistance of the Department of Justice, high schools in Des Moines, Iowa, are conducting a special course for 125 seniors on "The Science of Law Enforcement and Citizen Responsibility." In New York, Chicago and Cincinnati, the police are participating in the development of materials to be used by elementary school teachers in explaining to their pupils how to avoid dangerous situations and when and how to contact the police.

The Des Moines police are running a two and one-half month crime prevention course to educate the business community in how to cope effectively with robberies, burglaries, larcenies, worthless checks and vehicle thefts. Police in other cities sponsor robbery clinics for banks, savings and loan organizations and other firms that handle large amounts of money in the routine course of business. In Oakland, the police have distributed weekly bulletins to storeowners, including details about and pictures of bad-check artists or shoplifting rings operating around the city.

Crime prevention campaigns, if they involve a substantial segment of the community's residents and business people, in all probability can affect crime rates. To be effective, they must be built around up-to-date, accurate and specific crime prevention advice. Moreover, the specific needs of different groups in the community must be taken into account; for example, old people, young children, nighttime workers and neighborhood grocers all have different problems in terms of crime exposure. Appeals to each group should be individualized whenever possible; direct personal contact is superior to mere literature handouts. Social and professional groups can be an invaluable asset to the police in making the crime prevention message relevant to the interests of their members, and in turn such groups can help in getting the message over to the community as a whole.

Several communities haxe experimented successfully with concerted campaigns to impress upon all citizens the urgency of reporting promptly to the police all relevant information about crimes or suspicious incidents. In Chicago, a million citizens and 300 citizen-organizations are involved in "Operation Crime Stop." Members are asked to call the police about any suspicious happening and to report the nature of the incident, number, and description of the persons involved, and the license numbers of any cars used. Those citizens whose information leads to the solution or prevention of a crime are publicly honored each month. "Operation Crime Stop," inaugurated on April 13, 1964, is credited by the Chicago Police Department with assisting in 7,000 arrests.

The District of Columbia Police Department launched a "Signal Ten" program in December, 1966, to stimulate citizen aid to the police. The first step in this program was specifically directed against robberies. Thirty thousand leaflets were distributed to business firms; they provided the emergency police telephone number, instructions on how to react to an armed robbery, and space on the leaflet in which witnesses could write information on crimes they witnessed and sketch the offender's appearance.

Five hundred thousand small cards were also handed out to patrolmen for dispersal to robbery witnesses on the scene. They solicited the witnesses' names and requested that relevant information about the crime be noted on the card. Similar programs are now in operation in Chicago and New Orleans. A Florida sheriff's department has had good results with a junior deputy program that encourages youngsters to watch for and report suspicious incidents.

The police of San Diego city and county report that the "Stamp Out Crime Crusade," founded and financed by the Independent Insurance Agents Association of California in 1965, is making a notable contribution to local crime prevention efforts. Pointed toward increasing public awareness of crime problems and encouraging citizens to assist the police, the crusade was introduced statewide in California in 1966. After one year of operation in San Diego, Police Chief W. S. Sharp noted the program's success:

> The type of support and public awareness that the crusade has created is most welcome. Law enforcement in this city has felt its effects. In addition to a number of positive actions by citizens, we detect a swell of public support and cooperation that we have never known before.

In addition, Sheriff J. C. O'Connor of San Diego County noted:

> Where once the public all too often turned the other way, there is now a willingness to "stand up and be counted," and frequently in the face of great physical danger.

In some cities, taxicab fleets and utility company cars with their own radio communications systems have stepped forward and offered to serve as extra eyes and ears for the police. Kansas City, Missouri, has "Operation Barrier," an emergency alert program involving fourteen taxi, trucking and public utility firms with over 700 radio-equipped vehicles. A direct telephone network links police dispatchers with the agency dispatchers. Police emergency broadcasts can be relayed to private vehicles, and their drivers can assist the police in identifying and tracking down offenders, all at no cost to the city. The private vehicles check in periodically with the agency dispatcher for police information.

Birmingham, Chicago, Denver, Detroit, Green Bay and New Orleans also have routine arrangements for furnishing descriptions of missing or wanted persons by radio to taxicab drivers for lookout purposes. The District of Columbia police furnish descriptions of wanted persons or cars to the mobile equipment of the city's electric and gas companies and to the Bureau of Traffic Engineering and Operations. The effectiveness of these local liaison programs inspired a recent Congressional resolution to encourage direct radio communication between the police and taxicab drivers on a national scale.

The police of Oakland have attacked used car lot thefts and auto thefts from parking lots by a regulation making it compulsory for lot operators to construct sturdy barriers around the parking space. Passage of the ordinance followed a discovery that of all lots from which cars were stolen, 81 per cent had no protective barriers. The auto theft inspection service checks the applications and renewals of all parking lot owners for compliance and so far has reported universal cooperation.

Experience with building security codes has been very limited in this country. Yet they appear to hold a substantial potential for reducing housebreakings and burglaries. The only ordinance now in effect is in Oakland and it relates solely to exterior openings of commercial buildings, prescribing minimum security measure for all accessible vents. The security code is integrated with fire code requirements for easy exit, and the chief of police can require the installation of photoelectric, ultrasonic or other intrusion detection devices in buildings that have been burglarized frequently or that contain inventory of especially high value.

The Oakland police depend exclusively on voluntary adherence to the code even though the ordinance includes penalty provisions. But no prosecution has yet been instituted for its violation. The code was drawn up after concerted educational efforts by the police with the business community on preventive measures. The police there had found that of the 2,325 commercial burglaries in 1962, 52 per cent of the victims had been burglarized more than once in a single year; in 141 cases, three or more times. The business community was convinced that basic security provisions should be enacted into law.

The ordinance is now enforced in the following manner: a security section in the police department receives copies of all reports on burglaries and analyzes them to see if security defects are involved. It then sends an officer to talk with the owners and to recommend better security procedures. The case is followed up for compliance. As a continuing procedure, patrol officers who spot commercial building security defects also report them to the security section.

The department believes that its burglary prevention approach has been successful. It reports that in 1965, the increase in commercial burglaries was only 3.4 per cent as compared to 17.5 and 16.7 per cent increases in 1964 and 1963. During 1966, commercial burglaries increased only 2.3 per cent over 1965. Since the code was adopted, decreases of up to 75 per cent in burglaries are reported among complying businesses. Only 15 out of 1,092 business establishments contacted for security defects have refused to cooperate.

A successful property security code should ideally include provisions relative to residential as well as commercial property, and deal with lighting and internal security devices as well as with exterior openings. It would have to provide for administrative appeals and for ongoing enforcement checks by local officials familiar with building design, materials, and possible conflicts with other municipal codes relating to such matters as fire, safety and sanitation. The insurance industry should be intimately involved in its formulation so as to encourage compliance by lowering premiums. New construction should be reviewed and building permits and site inspections should be made to insure compliance. A model code developed for national use by construction experts, architects, municipal planners, fire prevention inspection personnel, police and insurance representatives would be an extremely worthwhile venture.

Short of legislation, it seems that reasonable security standards could be laid down by federal loan agencies as a requirement of new building financing. Federal banking agencies could insist on security features and up-to-date systems in all federally insured banks. Security requirements could also be made a standard feature of all public housing or urban renewal projects, federal or local. Limited experimentation should provide valuable experience for evaluating the efficiency and cost effectiveness of various types of security requirements and devices before they are translated into a universal legal requirement.

FIREARMS CONTROL LEGISLATION

The majority of the American public favors reasonable firearms control legislation. Since laws, as they now stand, do not effectively control the supply of firearms, legislative bodies at the federal, state and local levels should act to strengthen controls. Any legislative scheme should maximize the possibility of keeping firearms out of the hands of potential criminal offenders, while at the same time affording citizens ample opportunity to purchase such weapons for legitimate purposes.

It is appropriate to ban absolutely the sale of those weapons that no citizen has a justifiable reason for owning. And in addition, dangerous or potentially dangerous persons should be prohibited from purchasing firearms.

Finally, the prevention of crime and apprension of criminal offenders would be enhanced if each firearm were registered with a governmental jurisdiction. A record of ownership would aid the police in tracing and locating those who have committed or who threaten to commit violent crime. Law enforcement officers should know where each gun is and who owns it.

CITIZEN CRIME COMMISSIONS

Direct citizen action to support the police in the suppression and control of delinquency and crime has become an absolute necessity. In a number of instances, citizen crime commissions have provided forceful vehicles for proper and sustained citizen action.*

Citizen crime commissions can perform the essential function of coordinating the efforts of private groups within a community. They can work with the police to pinpoint problem areas where public education is most needed. They can see that the message reaches the groups most concerned. Such commissions can also serve as consulting agencies for individual groups or persons with specialized prevention problems.

Crime prevention education must also be sustained. Too often a crash campaign produces short-term reductions in certain kinds of crime and then loses momentum. Citizen efforts in this field can be extremely effective but they also need to be coordinated to insure complete coverage and continuing vigor.

---

*For an authoritative, interesting description of the American crime commission movement and an account of its organization, mission and history, see Ralph G. Murxy, *Crime Commission Handbook*, Baltimore, The Criminal Justice Commission, 1965.

It has been suggested that citizen's crime commissions or their counterpart is sufficiently important in community life to be coordinated on the state level by an official who would maintain a central depository of prevention material and experiences, run a clearing house for local commissions, and evaluate local programs. Former California Attorney General Stanley Mosk made such a suggestion in 1962:

> We have considered and discussed for some time, the possibility of a state-wide crime prevention coordinator . . . A formal state-wide bureau in the Department of Justice for the dissemination of information and educational materials on crime prevention and to assist in establishing local crime prevention councils could be most advantageous. Right now several agencies are handling this problem. A central depository and clearing house of such information would be most useful, not just for statistics, but for programmatic data too.

POLICE OPEN HOUSE

In an increasing number of jurisdictions, *Police Open House* has become an institution. Held annually, it is the occasion for the police to go "on parade" in renewing contact with the people they serve under the most favorable of auspices. It is good police work and the best of public relations.

It can be an educational experience not to be forgotten for the individual citizen and youngster. There is an aura that hovers above police service in terms of crime and the criminal, scientific crime detection and other aspects of the police operation that usually plays to an enthusiastic and overflow audience on these occasions. There is a certain fascination about a police officer and police work that is characteristic of no other profession that can be put to good use in courting the good will and support of the people in the community, both young and old.

Men in all walks of life, even presidents, are intrigued by the detective mystery thriller, detective feature series on television and front-page stories of major crimes, despite the fact that all of these present for the most part an inadequate image of the police. Any police officer will certify that these presentations, dramatized against a backdrop of murder and graft for the benefit of the gullible reader or listener, are seldom in agreement with the facts and fail to portray the challenging dimensions of police service in a modern social order. Police operations are infinitely more interesting than the year's best mystery thriller. An unequaled opportunity is here presented to give the youngsters a view "inside the lines" and an opportunity to gain a lasting impression of police service that could come from no other source. Here again, the doors are swung wide open to deliver the message concerning cooperation with the police and reducing the opportunity for the criminal offender to operate.

With the wealth of subject matter and materials at the disposal of the police, special displays can be prepared which speak for themselves in a language that can be understood by young and old alike. This is well illustrated by the following series of pictures which are reproduced through the courtesy of the Vancouver Police Department, Vancouver, British Columbia.

FIGURE 6. An introduction to the police traffic control function, portraying the role of the three E's—Education, Engineering and Enforcement. (Reproduced through the courtesy of Chief Constable J. R. Fisk, of the Vancouver Police Department, Vancouver, B. C.)

FIGURE 7. Here the opportunity is presented to impress upon members of the community, young and old, the critical importance of calling the police promptly upon observing a suspicious person or incident. (Reproduced through the courtesy of Chief Constable J. R. Fisk of the Vancouver Police Department, Vancouver, B. C.)

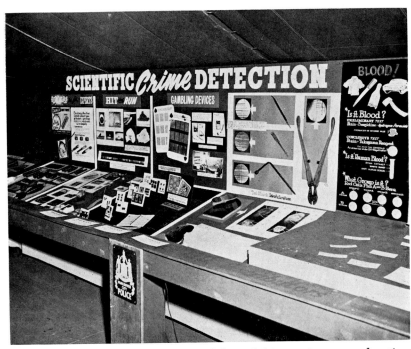

FIGURE 8.   The purchasing power of this exhibit requires no explanation. This is where the youngsters and the grown-ups will spend most of their time. (Reproduced through the courtesy of Chief Constable J. R. Fisk of the Vancouver Police Department, Vancouver, B. C.)

FIGURE 9. Police Open House can have a strong educational impact through stressing the role of the individual in reducing the opportunity to commit crime. (Reproduced through the courtesy of Chief Constable J. R. Fisk of the Vancouver Police Department, Vancouver, B. C.)

The foregoing illustrations do not include all of the photographs that were made available to the author by the Vancouver police. Depending upon the ingenuity and enthusiasm of the officer or officers involved, there is virtually no limit to the number and different types of displays that can be prepared.

Although detailed arrangements will vary from one department to another, visitors are usually conducted through the department in small groups by an experienced police officer, well qualified to explain in interesting and informative language the various phases of the police operation. The police experience no problem in gaining wide publicity in advance through the various news media concerning Open House, and newspaper and television reports usually give the event excellent coverage.

ROLE OF THE INDIVIDUAL CITIZEN

The individual citizen can play a strategic and effective role in reducing the opportunity to commit crime when he knows what to do, how to do it and is blessed with the urge to do it. Some of the rules he can use in promoting his safety and that of his family classify as just ordinary common sense; others are borne of police experience with crime and the criminal.

It is a major police responsibility to circulate the guidelines among the people they serve in an educational approach that will produce an awareness of potential danger and a consuming desire to do something about it. This is an area in which the liaison officer is favored with unlimited opportunities. It is to be kept in mind that reducing the opportunity for adult crime is also blocking off the path of invitation for the youngster who may not have yet made his first major mistake.

Many police departments have risen to the task in meeting this responsibility. The New York City Police Department recently gave citywide distribution to a pamphlet under the title, *Spare a Minute Mister? It Could Stop a Burglary—Your Own!* Its content is self-explanatory. (This pamphlet is reproduced on following pages, courtesy of the New York City Police Department.)

SPARE
A
MINUTE,
MISTER ?

IT
COULD
STOP
A
BURGLARY
— YOUR OWN!

During one recent, typical year in this city, more than 171,000 burglaries were reported to the police.

Of that total, approximately 50,000—or 30%—were burglaries of commercial premises. You, as the owner of a business, suffer some chance of becoming a burglary statistic.

Although we, the police, continue to stand between you and the would-be burglar, nothing short of a policeman guarding every storefront can *surely guarantee* your security, a financial impossibility.

There is, however, something that *you* can do—steps to be taken now to keep your premises off a burglar's roster of "easy marks."

Some of the following precautions are common sense; many, being quite technical, are not common knowledge; all have been culled from the practical experiences of policemen who specialize in burglary techniques and how to thwart them.

Give your attention now to avoid a statistic later.

LOOK TO

DOORS AND DOOR FRAMES

- Solid core doors are preferable to panel doors or doors with glass panes.
- Use metal sheets to line thin-paneled or hollow-cored doors.
- Exterior doors require non-removable hinge pins. Without these the entire door could be detached.
- If the door is sufficiently strong but the door frame is weak, use a lock that does not depend on the door frame for mounting or support.
- If "panic bars" are used on doors like those on theater fire doors, equip the

panic bar with an alarm that is activated when the door is opened by unauthorized persons during business hours.

GLASS DOORS

● Cover glass paneled doors with closely spaced steel bars or with strong mesh mounted on the inside.

● Install a lock which requires a key, and not simply a turnpiece, on glass doors that are opened from the inside. In the jargon of the locksmiths, the lock should be "keyed from within."

LOCKS

● Use door locks with deadbolt feature in conjunction with pick-resistant key cylinders, protected by a cylinder guard plate.

● Spring latches activated by slamming the door are inadequate.

● If a padlock is used, install pick-resistant type with a hardened shackle. Remove identification numbers from the padlock before use, including those on combination padlocks.

● Overhead doors require electric power or slide bolts and/or pick-resistant cylinder lock and guard plate.

● Equip elevator doors opening directly into offices or unguarded areas with key controlled locks for night use.

WINDOWS

● Secure windows with key-controlled in-side locks, ferry gates (accordion type), bars or mesh which cannot be removed from the outside. NOT APPLICABLE TO WINDOWS LEADING TO FIRE ESCAPES.

● Secure windows leading to fire escapes with devices approved by the New York City Board of Standards and Appeals.

- Non-removable hinge pins are recommended for windows with outside hinges.

TRANSOMS

- Use key-controlled inside lock, padlock, metal bars or mesh which cannot be removed from the outside.

HATCHWAYS

- Secure hatchways from the inside with sliding barrel bolts or heavy duty hook and eye.

- Protect openings larger than 12"x12" with bars or mesh.

METAL GATES AND BARS

- Equip accordion-type gates with top and bottom slide track, designed to prevent the gate from being pried from the bottom.

- Non-removable hinge pins are recommended for outside hinges.

- Round headed bolts are recommended on exterior bars, gates or mesh. Hex-headed bolts afford better protection when welded to the bar.

- Space bars not more than 5 inches apart.

LIGHTING

- Interior illumination is important, particularly at access points from rear and side alley doors.

- Place safes and cash registers in illuminated areas visible from the street.

- Leave cash registers open at night.

SAFES

- Chest-type safes (U.L. approved) are rec-

- ommended to protect valuables against burglary.

- Protect movable safe by detaching the wheels and anchoring the safe to the floor.

  If a combination safe is used:

  — Prevent manipulation by spinning the dial at least four times when locking the safe.

  — Change the combination when an employee with knowledge of the combination resigns or is discharged.

  — Do not leave a written copy of the combination on the premises.

KEYS

- Change the key cylinder whenever a key-holding employee is discharged or resigns, or when the key is lost.

- Limit the number of authorized personnel who may possess keys, and maintain key control by limiting the number of duplicates.

- If possible avoid using master-keyed locks.

- Pick-resistant key cylinders are recommended because duplication is more difficult.

CASH

- Record serial numbers of a few paper currency bills and intermingle them with working cash. This will provide evidence if cash is the object of a crime.

- Frequent cash deposits will minimize the risk of loss.

- If large amount of cash is required on premises for payroll or other purposes it should be placed in a safe or other secure receptacle until ready for distribution.

- Vary time of pick-up or delivery of cash.
- Vary the routes to and from the bank. Avoid remote areas.

CHECKS

- The immediate endorsement "for deposit only" with relevant identification data is recommended to prevent loss.
- Verify customer identification when accepting check in payment for cash-and-carry merchandise.
- Keep blank checks under lock and key when not in use.
- Check-writing machines are suggested to minimize alteration and forgery.

ALARM SYSTEMS

- A number of private companies manufacture, install and service different types of alarm systems. The choice would depend on the individual company's needs. An illustration of factors to consider in selecting an alarm system is:

  — An alarm which is deactivated by key in the control box located IN-SIDE the premises is preferable to an alarm which is deactivated from the outside.

EMPLOYEE PARTICIPATION

- Enlist the aid of employees in your security program. Encourage them to report suspicious persons or circumstances.
- Solicit employee suggestions for overall security.

FOR POLICE FIRE OR AMBULANCE IN CASE OF EMERGENCY DIAL 911

Police Department City of New York

JOHN V. LINDSAY
Mayor

PATRICK V. MURPHY
Commissioner

P.I.B. 74

The police department of Aurora, Illinois, recently distributed a pamphlet to the people of that community under the title, *Before You Leave On Your Vacation*. (This pamphlet, which appears on following pages, is reproduced, courtesy of the Aurora Police Department.)

A Public Service
of the
Aurora Police Department
9801 E. 16th Avenue   EM. 6-1551

VACATION

- ☐ Discontinue milk and newspapers. Notify dairy and publication offices — do not leave notes.

- ☐ Arrange with neighbor or relatives for removal of mail, handbills, etc.

- ☐ Notify your Police Department when you are leaving and when you will return.

- ☐ In addition, arrange with one or two neighbors to watch your house. Ask them to report any suspicious activities to the police.

- ☐ Protect your travel funds against loss or theft — use Travelers Checks.

- ☐ Be sure all range burners and oven are "OFF."

- ☐ Disconnect all radios, television, toasters, electric clocks and other appliances.

- ☐ Turn water heater "OFF."

- ☐ Be sure your oil or gas furnace is set to function properly during your absence.

- ☐ Make arrangements for care of pets.

- ☐ Leave house key with neighbor for periodic internal checks.

- ☐ Turn all electrical switches "OFF."

- ☐ Be sure all water faucets are turned off and all drains are open.

A PUBLIC SERVICE OF THE

✔ LIST

- ☐ Leave one or two lights burning, preferably one in the living room and one in the bathroom.

- ☐ Lock all doors and windows, including second floor windows.

- ☐ Do not leave valuables, jewelry and important papers in the house. Place them in a Safe Deposit Box.

- ☐ Latch and bar milk chute door.

- ☐ Arrange to have lawn mowed and watered regularly.

- ☐ Pull window shades down only half way.

- ☐ Remove perishable food and turn refrigerator to "LOW."

- ☐ Do not leave house keys under doormats or on window sills. Thieves know all the best hiding places.

- ☐ Take out rubbish and garbage.

- ☐ Secure tickets and reservations.

- ☐ Do last minute shopping.

- ☐ Leave destination address and telephone number with neighbor.

AURORA POLICE DEPARTMENT

What to Take

- ☐ First aid kit
- ☐ Flashlight
- ☐ Raincoats
- ☐ Sun glasses
- ☐ Pillows
- ☐ Travel iron
- ☐ Portable radio
- ☐ Address book
- ☐ Golf equipment
- ☐ Nail polish
- ☐ Comb — brushes
- ☐ Games, cards, etc.
- ☐ Blanket
- ☐ Thermos jug (water) — cup
- ☐ Camera — films
- ☐ Mending kit
- ☐ Safety pins
- ☐ Aspirin
- ☐ Stamps
- ☐ Fishing equipment
- ☐ Bathing suits

- ☐ Soap — towels
- ☐ Sweaters — jackets
- ☐ Paper — pen, pencil

IMPORTANT

- ☐ Car registration
- ☐ Drivers license
- ☐ Car insurance
- ☐ Route maps
- ☐ House keys
- ☐ Car tools checked
- ☐ Brakes checked
- ☐ Lights checked
- ☐ Check book
- ☐ Identification
- ☐ Duplicate car keys
- ☐ Credit cards

OTHERS

- ☐
- ☐
- ☐
- ☐

CHILDREN — They tire quickly. Take along toys or games — also blanket and pillow. *Be sure car doors are locked.* Don't forget thermos jug of water.

START EARLY — to avoid heavy local traffic.

DON'T OVERDO — Pull off road and rest if tired or sleepy. Do not chance an accident.

LOCK YOUR CAR — even if you are going to be away from it for only a short time. *Remove car keys* — leaving them in your car is an invitation to have it stolen.

PREVENT FIRES — Do not throw lighted cigars, cigarettes or pipe ashes out of car windows, particularly in wooded areas.

Be Careful -- Drive Safely

HAVE A GOOD TIME!

We will be glad to serve you further on your return.

Under the title, *A Message To Women,* the New York City Police Department distributed more than 100,000 copies of this pamphlet to Parent-Teacher Associations and women's groups and clubs throughout the city. It gives a list of do's and don'ts for women confronted with dangerous situations, such as loiterers near the home, intruders in the home, and precautions to be taken against burglars, muggers and molesters. A portion of the pamphlet is also devoted to hints for housewives in protecting their children. It emphasizes the need for remaining calm and for quick notification to the police in case of need. (This pamphlet is reproduced on the following pages, courtesy of the New York City Police Department.)

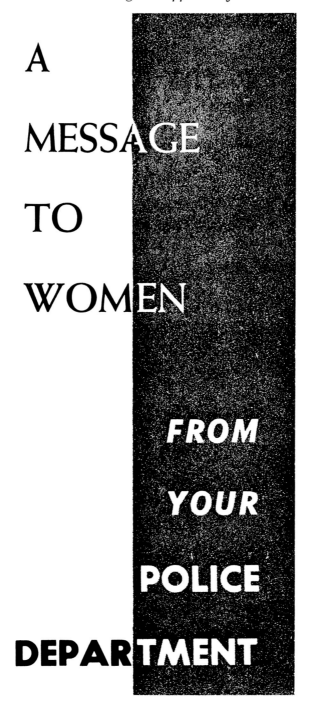

A

MESSAGE

TO

WOMEN

FROM

YOUR

POLICE

DEPARTMENT

For your protection

- Notify police promptly of any suspicious person loitering in the vicinity of your home or on routes that you ordinarily take. When travelling alone at night, walk where it's well lighted. Don't take short cuts.

- If awakened at night by an intruder, don't try to apprehend him. He might be armed. Do not panic. Lie still, observe carefully and at the first chance, call police.

- Never open the door automatically after a knock—insist that callers identify themselves. Install a window peephole.

- At night, double-lock your door and chain lock it, too. Equip your door with a lock which has a "dead bolt" as well as a spring lock.

- Install locks on windows so that they will be secure when open as well as closed.

- In case of burglary, don't enter residence if door has been forced. Don't touch anything. Notify police.

- If threatened by a robber, do as you are told. Observe as much as possible and notify police.

- Don't place keys under mats, in mail boxes or other receptacles outside the door.

- If you lose your doorkey, have locks changed immediately. Make certain your door is locked at all times. Some burglars make a career of finding open doors.

- Employ servants only on bonafide recommendation and after thorough investigation.

- When you go away, do it quietly. Be sure paper and milk deliveries are stopped in your absence. Don't leave notes.

- Don't flash sums of money in public places. Money and valuables belong in the bank. If you must keep them at home, don't display them. A safe that is hard to move is recommended.

- When shopping, don't leave your purse lying on a counter. Hold on to your shoulder bag at the lock. A pickpocket can open it unobserved in a crowded place. In a theatre, keep your bag on your lap. Don't place it on a seat.

Children need your protection

- Know the length of time it takes your child to walk to and from school.

- Immediately check any delay in arrival home.

- Know the safest route to and from school and instruct your children to follow that route.

- If your children are to arrive home after dark, arrange to meet them.

- Know your children's playmates and where they congregate.

- Instruct children to report to you suspicious persons or attempts by unknown adults to approach them or become friendly with them. Don't allow children to accept rides or gifts from anyone without your approval. Train children to check with you before going anywhere with anyone.

- Visit the school and become acquainted with teachers and school officials. You may learn of delinquent behavior before it becomes a serious problem.

- Be sure your baby sitter is a responsible person and capable of acting in an emergency.

- Report suspicious actions of adults in the vicinity of school yards and playgrounds.

You can help combat crime if you are aware of:

- Suspicious persons
- Questionable actions
- Dangerous conditions

Your information is valuable. Give it to the police quickly. Time is important. Look for these items.

- The individual's height, weight, age and complexion; his dress, speech, movements; any outstanding pecularities in appearance or actions. If there are two or more men, concentrate on one. Compare his physical proportions and age with someone you know.

- Distinguishing marks. A ring or other jewelry, tattoo or scar, missing tooth or finger, bowlegs or limp.

- The direction he took. If a car is used, the color, style and license number. If a license plate has several numbers, remember those that come first.

Call Police Headquarters by:

1. Dialing "O" for operator
2. Using police street telephone

Give your name
where you are
the nature of the incident

If emergency aid is needed, help will be dispatched immediately through the Police Department's two-way radio system.

PUBLIC INFORMATION BULLETIN No. 9

POLICE DEPARTMENT
CITY OF NEW YORK

ROBERT F. WAGNER   STEPHEN P. KENNEDY
     Mayor   Commissioner

This is the cover of brochure issued by
the Los Angeles Police Department.

Lady Beware!

The Los Angeles Police Department, because of budget limitations, was unable to supply the demand throughout the United
States for the pamphlet, *Lady Beware!** Its content follows:

---

*Reprinted courtesy of the Los Angeles Police Department.

LADY BEWARE

The city is a magnet for all types of people. Nearly all are law-abiding citizens; however, there is the exception who might endanger a woman like you. If you are home alone or travel unescorted, you should be aware of measures you can use to safeguard yourself from this type of person.

Walking

A man determined to follow and attack a woman is more readily attracted to a woman who is wearing revealing clothes or behaving in a suggestive manner.

After getting off a bus at night, look around to see whether you are being followed. If someone suspicious is behind you, cross the street. Should he continue to trail you, be prepared to defend yourself by . . .

- Screaming and running to a lighted residence or business.
- Flagging down a passing car.
- Using any available object for a weapon such as a nail file, high-heeled shoe or an umbrella.

Do not be tempted to accept rides from strangers. If a car approaches you and you are threatened, scream and run in a direction opposite that of the car. The driver will have to turn around to pursue you.

Maintain a secure grip on your purse, preferably under your arm. Money and wallets are safer in an inside pocket. Unless absolutely necessary, never carry expensive jewelry or large amounts of money.

Walk near the curb and avoid passing close to shrubbery, dark doorways and other places of concealment. Shun shortcuts.

Have your key ready so your house door can be opened immediately.

When arriving at home by taxi or private auto, request the driver to wait until you are inside.

Driving

When practicable, travel on well-lighted busy streets. Keep windows rolled up and doors locked.

Do not leave your purse on the seat. Put it in the glove compartment or on the floor opposite yourself. Your purse can lure a criminal to your car.

Keep your car in gear while halted at traffic lights and stop signs. If your safety is threatened, hold down on the horn and drive away as soon as possible.

If you believe you are being followed by another car, do not drive into your driveway. Should another car attempt to force you to the side of the road, do not pull over. In both instances, obtain the license number and "WRITE IT DOWN" along with any description; then continue to a police station or open business. Report the incident to the police.

Should your car become disabled in an isolated area, raise the hood and sit inside with the doors locked until assistance arrives. Leave the windows up while you talk to whomever approaches. It may be preferable to remain there rather than go with strangers to seek help. Frequently freeways are patrolled at all hours.

When traveling alone, you should not stop to aid disabled motorists.

Park only in a well-lighted spot near enough to your destination for safety. Look around for loiterers before leaving the car.

Lock your car whenever you leave it. This will help safeguard property inside and discourage thieves. Upon your return, examine behind the front seat before you enter the car. A criminal may have entered to wait for you.

Upon arriving at home, keep the headlights on until the garage is opened, the car is parked and the house door is unlocked. Be particularly, alert when going into apartment house basement garages. If possible, have a friend or relative meet you.

A well-lighted garage and front door entrance is a friend to an unescorted woman.

At Home

Women who live alone should list only their last names and initials in phone directories and on mailboxes.

After moving into a new house or apartment, it is a good idea to change the door locks. Previous tenants or former employees may still have keys. Pin-tumbler or square bolt types are best for replacement as these are quite difficult to force.

Install and use chain locks or a peep-hole. When alone, you should never open a door to strangers without having the chain in place.

Police officers will display credentials whenever asked. You should always request salesmen and repairmen to show identification prior to being admitted.

Be alert to protect your neighbors as well as yourself. Never mention to a stranger that a neighbor lives alone or is at home alone.

When a stranger asks to use your phone, do not permit him to enter. Offer to summon emergency assistance or make the call for him.

Should wrong number calls be received, never reveal your name or address or admit you are alone. Do not give your phone number to an unknown caller, but ask what number he is calling. Do not prolong the conversation. Hang up. Notify the police of obscene calls.

Keep windows secured or install window locks on those left open for ventilation. These can limit openings to space small enough to prevent entry.

Window shades should be drawn after dark. Leave lights on in two or more rooms to indicate presence of other persons.

Be cautious about entering an apartment house elevator with strange men. It is wiser to remain in the lobby for a few minutes.

When using a laundry room in an apartment house, never remain there alone. Women have been assaulted in such areas.

If you are thinking about the use of a gun for protection, you must be aware of the hazards involved. Consult now with officers at your local police station. Remember, if the criminal has the opportunity, he might take the gun away to use against you.

Your best defense is prolonged loud screaming. A good protective device is an electric buzzer which you can have installed to alert your neighbor in the event of an emergency.

If a door or window has been forced or broken while you were absent . . . "DO NOT ENTER OR CALL OUT." Someone may still

be inside. Use a neighbor's phone immediately to call the police and wait outside until they arrive.

Never assume that suspicious persons, occurrences or vehicles have been reported to the police. Do it yourself at once. Keep the police department number by your telephone.

Call whenever danger threatens. In the event of a false alarm it is better to be a bit embarrassed than to be killed or injured.

If Attacked ...

No holds are barred when your safety is threatened.

Cries for help have discouraged many criminals and often resulted in their capture.

THE EDUCATIONAL APPROACH

The following material indicates again the educational approach that the police can use effectively in alerting the people of the community to take certain precautionary measures that will reduce the opportunity.*

Always call the police IMMEDIATELY when you see a crime being committed.

There are other times when the police should be called and notified of things that are happening. That stranger who is "taking a shortcut" through your backyard might have just robbed one of your neighbors and is attempting to get away.

That minor fight next door might be the beginning of a violent crime. Getting the police there early could prevent a great deal of pain and suffering—or even **save someone's life!**

Do not be hesitant to call for fear of reporting something that amounts to nothing. For example, one person saw several suspicious individuals near a parked car, as he drove by. His call to the police saved a neighbor from having his car stolen.

Also, what might appear to be an **illegally** parked car could be just the information needed by the police to return a stolen car to its rightful owner.

Learn the fine nuance between helping your neighbor and interfering in his business.

Talk with your neighbors about the crime problem and crime

*Reproduced through the courtesy of Clarence O. Huse, Editorial Department, *The Plain Truth*, Ambassador College, Pasadena, California, 1970.

prevention. Let them know how you feel about the problem. **Discuss** *joint cooperation* in keeping a vigil on each other's apartments or homes.

Perhaps you want to work up a code of some kind which would inform the other neighbors when one is having his home burglarized.

Neighbors who know each other; who are cooperating in a joint effort to keep crime down in their area—make a neighborhood **more secure** from the threat of crime.

When You Encounter a Burglar

If you hear or see a prowler on your own or a neighbor's property at night . . . **do not turn a light on or call out.** Notify the police and let them determine his business. Do not become impatient when the police seem slow to respond. They will approach silently and attempt to cut off avenues of escape.

Remain on the telephone, if possible, and report any changes in the prowler's actions. Obtain his description. Do not open your door to anyone except a police officer who has identified himself.

If you observe suspicious persons or occurrences, do not assume that the police have already been summoned. Do it yourself immediately. Keep the Police Department number by your telephone. Memorize it. In an emergency you can dial the operator—she can connect you with the police department. Many communities have a special three-digit number to call in such emergencies.

Write down the license numbers of vehicles used by suspicious persons in your neighborhood.

But suppose you suddenly discover a burglar has already entered your home? What can you do then?

Your best course is to lie quietly and do *nothing*. Most burglars are armed, "high" on drugs, or at a dangerous emotional pitch.

Don't endanger your family. Let the burglar take what he wants and leave. You may not have silverware at breakfast in the morning, but you and your family will all be present at the table.

There is one exception to this general rule. If you are upstairs, and the burglar is downstairs, lock your door and use your best weapon—**noise!** If there is a phone in your bedroom, use it! Call the police!

If not, here's where **neighbor contact** is so important. If you have some pre-arranged signal—such as tapping on a pipe, banging on the wall, a loud blaring radio, some kind of piercing alarm you can turn on—then your neighbors can assist you by calling the police and carefully coming to your assistance.

If you suddenly find a rapist in your home and are **unable** to contact police—try to let neighbors know of your plight.

Also, turn on the lights—and **scream!** This is a woman's best weapon. Although this is a terrible thought to contemplate, you may have to grapple with your assailant.

It **cannot** be recommended that you try to *injure* your attacker for several reasons. One very practical reason is this. Suppose you were to try to use a knife to stab him. If you missed—and the chances are you would—this could so **enrage or frighten** him, that he might kill you.

Put up a vicious struggle, scream—but leave your attacker a *means of escape*. In that way, he will think more about escaping than harming you.

Common Sense Rules

Keep lights burning during the nighttime at front and rear doors whether you are at home or away.

Be alert in protecting not only your own house or apartment, but your neighbor's as well. *Don't tell a stranger* that your neighbor is not at home.

Women who live alone should list only their *last names* and initials in phone directories and on mailboxes.

Apartment dwellers should report suspicious persons to the manager or the police. Most apartment burglars work in the daytime.

Managers or other apartment house employees should periodically check basement garages or parking areas for strangers or vehicles which do not belong there. Note vehicle make, color, model, and license number. If the vehicle contains items such as a television, radios, or other appliances, notify the police immediately.

Do not keep large sums of money, expensive jewelry, or other valuables at home when not necessary. Rent a safe deposit box. Jewelry should be photographed for identification.

Cash *should not be "hidden"* in sugar bowls, bureau drawers, or behind pictures. Thieves know enough to look in these and other apparently secret places. Coin banks are also easy targets.

Maintain a record of the serial numbers and model numbers of firearms, appliances, tools, and other equipment or mark them so they can be identified. Your vehicle license plate number or the serial number of your operator's license could be used as an identification mark on items that lack other numbers.

In many instances, stolen furs cannot be returned to the rightful owners when the labels and linings are missing. Place identifying marks in several places on the insides of the skins.

Discourage Burglars

After you move into a house, it is a good idea to *have the tumblers of the locks reset.* Previous tenants or employees may have keys in their possession. If you move into a housing project, it also might be a good idea to reset the locks. Many of those projects *mass-produce* keys of the same kind for each house.

Pin-tumbler locks on all outside doors offer the most protection. But pin-tumbler locks should always be accompanied by dead bolt locks in case the criminal can pick the primary lock. Doors with *glass* panels should also have double cylinder locks which require keys on the inside, but be sure locks don't trap you inside in case of fire.

Exterior doors which open outward should be installed with hinges of a type where the pins cannot be removed. (Such hinges are stamped "NPD"—non-removable pins.) *Slide bolts and chains* on the inside of all outer doors are an inexpensive investment, but never rely on chains for your *only* lock. Many criminals can neatly and silently disengage a chain lock. Remember, locks that you can open with a skeleton key can also be opened by anyone who buys such keys at a hardware store.

Some people will say, "But locks and alarm systems are too expensive. I can't *afford* them."

But how *valuable* is your life or the lives of your loved ones? The truth is you can't afford **not** to get burglar-proof locks. You may need to do **without** some pleasures and use that money to make your home *secure!*

Door molding should be tight in areas of mortise locks to prevent them from being shimmed with a flat piece of celluloid or other device. Driving a row of small head nails through the molding in a vertical line about eight inches long in the area of the latch will help, or, shimproof locks which have two moving parts in the latch may be installed.

Sliding glass doors and windows are easily forced. By placing a piece of wood (a broomstick will do) in the bottom track, movement is prevented.

A latched window screen is no guarantee of protection. Lock the windows or install window locks on those which are left open for ventilation. These can limit openings to spaces small enough to forestall entry.

Safety locks should be installed on *louvered windows* as these types may be pried with ease. Supplementary locks are recommended for windows that face onto fire escapes.

Shrubbery, stacked lawn furniture, or any other material that obscures doors or windows can afford concealment to a burglar while he breaks in. Regular storage of such items and properly trimmed greenery would eliminate this advantage.

Check with your local locksmith for his recommendations. Do it as soon as possible.

Keep *ladders* locked up or chained while not in use. Suggest that your neighbors do the same. *Garages* should be locked to prevent burglars from using your own tools to break into your home.

While at Home . . .

Refrain from automatically opening the door whenever the doorbell rings. If you do not have a *chain lock* or a *peephole* installed on the door, insist that the visitor call out his identification.

Demand credentials before admitting salesmen or repairmen, particularly if you have not requested their appearance. Refuse to deal with any caller of this type who does not present credentials. Notify the police.

Outside doors should be kept locked at all times. Some thieves look for residents who are working in the yard, hanging up laundry or otherwise engaged outside. Then they approach from an opposite side of the building and enter through an unlocked door to steal purses, money, or other valuable items. These occurrences are very common and frequently the loss is not discovered until some time later. Even then, owners do not always make a report to the police as they believe the property might only be mislaid.

If wrong number telephone calls are being received continually, report them to the police. Do not reveal your own phone number or address to unknown callers and never admit to them that you are alone.

Here's one way to handle a caller. *Caller:* "Who is this?" *Your response:* "Whom are you *calling?*"

Be sure you *do not give* your name unless you are completely satisfied as to the caller's identity. Don't say this is "Marge."

Burglars or sex criminals use telephones, claiming to be "repairmen" or survey takers. Often, when someone answers, they just say, "Sorry, wrong number."

If you receive such a call, notify police—a burglar may be "working" a certain area of the city, and such information may help in apprehending him. Obviously, late-night calls from strangers, or "wrong numbers" and the like would be suspicious calls. Treat them as such. Be alert to the possibilities. When a stranger asks to use your telephone, do not permit him to enter. Offer to make the call for him or summon police assistance if he so requests.

Be sure any alarm system you have (it's a good idea to install one) has been turned on before you retire for the night.

On occasions when guests use a room for storage of coats and purses be certain the windows are securely fastened and the blinds completely closed. A slightly open window will permit someone to manipulate a long pole from the outside to obtain the property.

Upon retiring for the night do not leave your valuables in exposed locations. The purse currently being used should be placed in a concealed location. Remove wallets from pants left near the bedside.

Make A SAFETY CHECK every night before retiring! Be sure all doors and windows are locked and proper lights are on.

In the event a burglar gains entrance to your home at night while you are in bed, quietly telephone the police *if it is completey safe to do so.* Remain calm. Tell the police operator your address, what is happening, and where you are in the house if you are unable to get out.

Some authorities recommend a "security room." It would have a separate telephone receiver and line. Also, it could be locked securely. From this room, if approached by a burglar, you could call out, "I've already called the police."

Apartments or homes with more than one door are best to live in. Then you can more easily *escape,* if a burglar gains entrance.

Use of a firearm or lethal weapon to defend yourself against a burglar or other felon cannot be recommended. *Most burglars are armed!* Besides, if the criminal is not armed, he might take your weapon away to use against you. Also, you may accidentally shoot someone of your own family. When the burglar shoots he has no such worry.

There is not even any protection from the law if you shoot at prowlers or Peeping Toms. They are guilty of misdemeanors only, as long as they do not enter a house or other structure.

In summary, do not use guns. Be silent, unless you are in a "secure" room, or unless you are being personally attacked.

Away From Home . . .

A residence which presents a lived-in appearance is a deterrent to burglars. Never leave notes which can inform a burglar that your house is unoccupied. Make certain all windows and doors are secured before departure. An empty garage advertises your absence, so close the doors.

When going out at night, leave one or more interior lights on and perhaps have a radio playing—but not too loud. Timers may be purchased that will turn lights on and off during your absence.

Do not leave door keys under flower pots or doormats, inside an unlocked mailbox, over the doorway, or in other obvious places. Burglars usually look in these places first. Valuable clothing, rugs, or furs should not be left on the line while you are away from home.

When Planning Prolonged Absences

Discontinue milk, newspaper, and other deliveries by phone or in person ahead of time. Do not leave notes.

Arrange for lawn care and have someone remove advertising circulars and other debris regularly. Notify the post office to hold or forward your mail. Perhaps, have a trustworthy person pick it up daily. Apartment house tenants could also heed this hint as stuffed mail receptacles are a giveaway that no one is home.

Inform neighbors of your absence so they can be extra alert for suspicious persons. Leave a key with them so your place may be periodically inspected. Direct them to vary the positions of your shades and blinds. Tightly drawn blinds are a sign that the residence is not occupied.

Do not have the telephone temporarily disconnected. This is another giveaway that occupants are out for an extended period of time. Be sure to turn loudness of ring down so it cannot be used as a cue that no one is home.

When you leave, do not publicize your plans. Some burglars specialize in reading newspaper accounts of other people's vacation activities.

Contact your local police division and inform them of your proposed absence, how long you will be gone and where you can be reached. Special attention will be given to the premises while you are away.

If you find a door or window has been forced or broken while you were absent . . . **do not enter.** The criminal may still be inside. Use a neighbor's phone immediately to summon police. Do not touch anything or clean up if a crime has occurred. Preserve the scene until the police can inspect for evidence.

You and Your Automobile

Before entering your car, look into the back seat. This *especially* applies to girls and women who could be abducted by a sex deviate. But **everyone** should beware!

While driving, keep doors locked and windows rolled up. A convertible with the top down spells trouble.

Never give a ride to anyone! Also, *never hitchhike* yourself.

Keep alert at all times for possible danger situations. Always leave yourself enough room to maneuver your car out of a potential problem situation.

When you park your car, try to leave it in a well-lighted area. *DON'T LEAVE YOUR KEYS IN THE CAR!* And don't "hide" an extra set of keys under the fender or some such place. Professional car thieves look in these places first.

Lock your car. If you leave it unlocked, you're inviting a potential thief to steal your car.

A professional thief may still break into your car if it is locked. The best protection against him is to install 50-cent extra ignition switch locked in the glove compartment. This prevents "hot-wiring" your car. In most cases, however, locked doors *and* "wing windows" prevent theft.

Don't leave valuables in the car or the glove compartment. Do not leave an expensive object such as a camera visible—it's very tempting for anyone passing by.

A final word.

While driving, if you happen to see what looks like a stalled car—**never stop to assist!** Call the police. They will be happy to see what the trouble is. A "help needed" situation may just be a plant for a robbery.

When You're Out Walking

Avoid dark and deserted places. Stay away from neighborhoods and parts of town known to be dangerous. Recently, a girl was raped in a park while her boyfriend was pinned down and beaten. They had just been told by police to **stay out** of the area.

Use common sense! Stay away from potential trouble.

When walking, stay away from buildings and walk next to the street. A thug lurking in hallways or alleys could pull you in if you are too close to buildings.

Be alert. If you see suspicious persons, avoid them. Walk on the other side of the street if necessary.

Don't carry large amounts of cash. This is very important when you are on a trip or vacation. Use traveler's checks. Have a full inventory of your credit cards. If they're stolen, you can immediately report the details to the proper office.

Pickpockets are a problem in crowded urban areas. Always be aware of your wallet. If jostled, immediately check to see that nothing has been stolen. Don't assume your wallet is safe in your inside coat pocket. Professional pickpockets can "lift" it from any pocket. Be alert.

You also need to protect yourself against purse snatchers. This type of thief preys on elderly women who are incapable of defending themselves.

The caution of staying out of dangerous and unlit areas applies with great force here. Also, **never** leave your purse on a seat, in a ladies' room, or elsewhere, unattended. Hold on to your purse. This is the greatest protection you can offer yourself.

If you are a victim of a purse snatching, the greatest asset a woman has is a sharp, piercing **scream.** The thief may drop the purse and run like a scared rabbit.

Actually, a woman's scream is her *best protective device* in **any** situation she may encounter from a burglary to a potential rape.

The carrying of weapons on one's person is not recommended by authorities. "*Every law enforcement agency* is in agreement that it is best not to carry any weapon." (From a protection booklet, *Operation On Guard*, issued by the Los Angeles County District Attorney's office.)

Protect Your Children

Know where your children are at all times! This common sense rule is broken all too often. Its violation is the **cause** for many a heartbreaking situation.

Infants and young children at home should be within eyeshot of the parent. Take your children to school. Arrange to meet them when school is out. Don't allow your young children to roam the streets by themselves.

Teach children **not** to go to strangers and to report suspicious persons to you, teachers or policemen. *Teach your children that a policeman is their greatest friend outside the home!*

Instruct your children **against** loitering in public places. Do not allow them out after dark by themselves.

Also, a high percentage of child molestations are caused by **friends and blood relatives.** As distasteful as this may sound, it is a hard fact of life. Be sure you know the character of people who might keep your children overnight, for a visit or on a trip.

There will be times when you need a baby-sitter. Take great care in the selection of one. Remember, that sitter is now in **your** place as a guardian of your precious children. Insist that the baby-sitter take the **same precautions** as you do. Be sure that she is aware of every security protection item mentioned in this booklet. Make it clear *how important* they are!

Take her on a security tour of the house; instruct her on not admitting strangers; give her the phone number where you can be reached. Explain how to reach the police. In short, educate your baby-sitter so that she will be able to handle a potential problem in the same way as you would.

And, concerning your teen-age children:

Know the person your daughter or son is dating. Don't let either go out with people that are strangers to you. Insist on getting to know those they date.

Today's teen-age girls have their own special problems.

J. Edgar Hoover, director of the Federal Bureau of Investigation, has formulated a no-nonsense code he feels will help young girls steer clear of danger. Here it is as it appeared in the *Chicago Tribune.*

1. If any stranger—or even a slight acquaintance—makes improper advances, tell your parents immediately. Too often, young people dislike the idea of getting someone into trouble. Just remember that if you don't report him, he probably will get into worse trouble later on—to say nothing of the harm he may cause.

2. If you know of any pornographic pictures or literature being passed around, notify your parents immediately. Collecting obscene reading matter is a favorite habit of degenerates. If the authorities

can run down the source, they may be able to rid the community of danger before it starts.

3. Know your date! Don't go on blind dates.

4. Stay out of lovers' lanes. They're favorite haunts of sex criminals. [And, these are not places where upstanding, moral teen-agers—who know the deep responsibility of dating, sex and marriage—ought to be anyway.]

5. Don't wander away alone from the crowd at picnics and outings. Sex criminals are attracted to groups of young people and, given an opportunity, can strike with frightening speed.

6. Dress sensibly. Don't ask for trouble.

7. Be civil to strangers who ask directions, but never go part way with them. The "directions trick" is a favoriate among deviates. They count on the natural helpfulness of young people.

8. Be careful about accepting work from a stranger. This is another insidious dodge. Always make sure that the person offering employment is a respectable businessman.

9. Don't go around the house half-dressed. It's an invitation to Peeping Toms and worse.

10. Never hitchhike! And never pick up a hitchhiker.

Get to know your children. Do more things at home with them. The more they are in the sanctity and protection of the home, the less the chance for some disaster to strike.

Follow these common-sense rules! If you do, your chances or your loved ones' chances of being a crime victim will be greatly reduced.

BIBLIOGRAPHY

AICHORN, AUGUST. *Delinquency and Child Guidance.* New York, International Universities Press, 1964.

AMOS, WILLIAM E., AND WELLFORD, CHARLES P. *Delinquency Prevention: Theory and Practice.* Englewood Cliffs, Prentice-Hall, 1967.

ASHENHUST, PAUL H. *Police and the People.* Springfield, Thomas, 1956.

AUBREY, ARTHUR S., JR. *The Officer in the Small Department.* Springfield, Thomas, 1961.

BARNES, HARRY E., AND TEETERS, NEGLEY K. *New Horizons in Criminology.*

BECCARIA, CAESAR BONESANA. *An Essay on Crimes and Punishments.* English translation by Edward D. Ingraham. Philadelphia, Philip H. Nicklin, 1819.

BLOCK, HARRY E., AND FLYNN, FRANK T. *Delinquency: The Juvenile Offender in America Today.* New York, Random House, 1956.

BRISTOW, ALLEN P. *Effective Police Manpower Utilization.* Springfield, Thomas, 1969.

BRANDSTATTER, A. F., AND RADELET, LOUIS A. *The Police and Community Relations.* Beverly Hills, Glencoe, 1968.

BROWN, THORVALD T. *The Enigma of Drug Addiction.* Springfield, Thomas, 1961.

BURT, CYRIL. *The Young Delinquent.* New York, D. Appleton-Century, 1938.

CARR, LOWELL J. *Delinquency Control.* New York, Harper & Bros., 1941.

CHAPMAN, SAMUEL G. *Police Patrol Readings,* 2nd ed. Springfield, Thomas, 1970.

CLIFT, RAYMOND E. *A Guide to Modern Police Thinking,* 2nd ed. Cincinnati, W. H. Anderson, 1965.

CLOWARD, RICHARD A., AND OHLIN, LLOYD E. *Delinquency and Opportunity.* New York, Free Press, 1960.

CURRY, J. E., AND KING, GLEN D. *Race Tensions and the Police.* Springfield, Thomas, 1962.

DAHL, RAYMOND A., AND BOYLE, HOWARD H. *Arrest, Search and Seizure.* (Supplement) Milwaukee, Hammersmith-Courtney, 1967.

DAILEY, JOHN T. *Evaluation of the Contribution of Special Programs in the Washington, D. C. Schools to the Prediction and Prevention of Delinquency.* Washington, U. S. Office of Education, 1966.

DIENSTEIN, WILLIAM. *How to Write a Narrative Investigation Report.* Springfield, Thomas, 1969.

DOUGHERTY, EDWARD. *Safety in Police Pursuit Driving.* Springfield. Thomas, 1961.

188

DUDYCHA, GEORGE J. *Psychology for Law Enforcement Officers*. Spring-field, Thomas, 1960.

EARLE, HOWARD H. *Student Instructor Guide on Police-Community Relations*. Springfield, Thomas, 1970.

FEDERAL BUREAU OF INVESTIGATION. *Uniform Crime Reports*. Washington, U. S. Gov. Print. Off., 1969 and 1970.

FERRI, ENRICO. *Criminal Sociology*. New York, D. Appleton-Century, 1896.

FIELD, ANNITA T. *Fingerprint Handbook*. Springfield, Thomas, 1959.

GAMMAGE, ALLEN Z. *Basic Police Report Writing*. Springfield, Thomas, 1970.

GARAFOLO, RAFFAELE. *Criminology*. Translated by Robert W. Millar, Montclair, N. J., 1968; written 1886.

GAULT, ROBERT H. *Criminology*. New York, D. C. Heath, 1932.

GERBER, SAMUEL R., AND SCHROEDER, OLIVER. *Criminal Investigation*. Cincinati, W. H. Anderson, 1962.

GIALLOMBARDO, ROSE. *Juvenile Delinquency*. New York, John Wiley & Sons, 1968.

GIBBONS, DON C. *Changing the Lawbreaker*. Englewood Cliffs, Prentice-Hall, 1965.

GILSTON, DAVID H., AND PODELL, LAWRENCE. *The Practical Patrolman*. Springfield, Thomas, 1959.

GLUECK, SHELDON AND ELEANOR. *Criminal Careers*. New York, O. A. Knopf, 1930.

————*Criminal Careers in Retrospect*. New York, Commonwealth Fund, 1943.

————*Delinquency and Non-Delinquency, in Retrospect*. Cambridge, Harvard, 1968.

————*Delinquents in the Making*. New York, Harper & Bros., 1952.

————*Family Environment and Delinquency*. Boston, Houghton, Mifflin, 1962.

————*500 Criminal Careers*. New York, O. A. Knopf, 1930.

————*500 Delinquent Women*. New York, O. A. Knopf, 1963.

————*Juvenile Delinquents Grown Up*. New York, London, Oxford U. P., 1940.

————*Later Criminal Careers*. New York, Krans Reprint, 1966.

————*Unraveling Juvenile Delinquency*. Cambridge, Harvard, 1951.

————*Predicting Delinquency and Crime*. Cambridge, Harvard, 1959.

————*1,000 Juvenile Delinquents*. Cambridge, Harvard, 1965.

————*Preventing Crime*. New York, McGraw-Hill, 1936.

————*Ventures in Criminology*. Cambridge, Harvard, 1964.

GOCKE, B. W. *Police Sergeants Manual*. Los Angeles, O. W. Smith Book, 1943.

GOURLEY, C. DOUGLAS, AND BRISTOW, ALLEN P. *Patrol Administration*. Springfield, Thomas, 1961.

GOURLEY, C. DOUGLAS. *Public Relations and the Police.* Springfield, Thomas, 1953.

HARNEY, MALACHI L., AND CROSS, JOHN C. *The Narcotic Officer's Notebook.* Springfield, Thomas, 1961.

HAZELET, JOHN C. *Police Report Writing.* Springfield, Thomas, 1960.

HEALY, WILLIAM, AND BRONNER, AUGUSTA. *The Individual Delinquent.* Boston, Little, Brown, 1915.

HEALY, WILLIAM, AND BRONNER, AUGUSTA. *Delinquents and Criminals.* New York, MacMillan, 1926.

HIGGINS, LOUIS L. *Policewoman's Manual.* Springfield, Thomas, 1961.

HOLMAN, MARY. *The Police Officer and the Child.* Springfield, Thomas, 1962.

HOOTON, ARNEST. *The American Criminal: An Anthropological Study.* Cambridge, Harvard, 1939.

HOUTS, MARSHALL. *From Arrest to Release.* Springfield, Thomas, 1958.

———*The Rules of Evidence.* Springfield, Thomas, 1956.

———*From Evidence to Proof.* Springfield, Thomas, 1956.

INTERNATIONAL CITY MANAGERS ASSOCIATION. *Municipal Police Administration,* 6th ed., Chicago, The Association, 1969.

KENNEY, JOHN P., AND WILLIAMS, JOHN B. *Police Operations: Policies and Procedures.* Springfield, Thomas, 1961.

KENNEY, JOHN P., AND PURSUIT, DAN G. *Police Work With Juveniles and the Administration of Juvenile Justice.* 4th ed., Springfield, Thomas, 1970.

KING, EVERETT M. *The Officer Speaks in Public.* Springfield, Thomas, 1958.

———*The Auxiliary Police Unit.* Springfield, Thomas, 1960.

KING, GLEN D. *First Line Supervisor's Manual.* Springfield, Thomas, 1961.

KVARACEUS, WILLIAM C. et al. *Delinquent Behavior: Principles and Practices.* Washington, N. E. A., 1959.

LaFAVE, WAYNE R. *Arrest: The Decision to Take a Suspect Into Custody.* Boston, Little-Brown, 1965.

LANGFORD, BERYL; SHEEHAN, ROBERT; LOBKOVISH, THOMAS F., AND WATSON, PAUL J. *Stopping Vehicles and Occupant Control.* Springfield, Thomas, 1960.

LEONARD, V. A. *The Police, the Judiciary and the Criminal.* Springfield, Thomas, 1969.

LEONARD, V. A., AND MORE, HARRY W., JR. *Police Organization and Management,* 3rd ed., Mineola, N. Y., Foundation Press, 1971.

MacIVER, ROBERT M. *The Prevention and Control of Delinquency.* New York, Atherton, 1967.

MYREN, RICHARD A. Processing and reporting of police offenders, in Southwestern Law Enforcement Institute: *Institute on Juvenile Delinquency.* Dallas, Southwestern Legal Foundation, 1962.

NELSON, A. T., AND SMITH, HOWARD E. *Car Clouting: The Crime, The Criminal and The Police.* Springfield, Thomas, 1958.

O'Connor, George W., and Watson, Nelson A. *Juvenile Delinquency and Youth Crime: The Police Role.* Washington, Int. Assoc. of Chiefs of Police, 1964.

Osborn, Frederick. *The Future of Human Heredity.* New York, Weybright & Tally, 1969.

Penofsky, Daniel J. *Guidelines for Interrogation.* Rochester, Jurisprudence, 1967.

Pennsylvania Department of Public Instruction. *A Guide for Cooperation Between School Officers and the Police.* Harrisburg, 1968.

Perkins, Rollin. *Criminal Law and Procedure.* Mineola, N. Y., Foundation Press, 1959.

Porterfield, Austin L. *Youth in Trouble.* The Leo Potishman Foundation, Texas Christian University, Fort Worth, 1946.

Post, Richard S., and Kingsbury, Arthur A. *Security Administration: An Introduction.* Springfield, Thomas, 1970.

President's Commission on Law Enforcement and Administration of Justice: U. S. Government Printing Office, Washington, D. C.
   The Challenge of Crime in a Free Society. 1967.
   Task Force Report: Juvenile Delinquency and Youth Crime. 1967.
   Task Force Report: The Police. 1967.
   Task Force Report: Science and Technology. 1967.
   Task Force Report: Organized Crime. 1967.
   Task Force Report: Crime and Its Impact, An Assessment. 1967.

Reckless, Walter C. *The Crime Problem.* New York, D. Appleton-Century, 1950.
———*The Etiology of Delinquent and Criminal Behavior.* New York, Social Science Research Council, 1943.
———*Criminal Behavior.* New York, McGraw-Hill, 1940.
———and Smith. *Juvenile Delinquency,* New York, McGraw-Hill, 1932.

Robinson, Sophia M. *Juvenile Delinquency—Its Nature and Control.* New York, Harper & Bros., 1960.

Schwarz, John I. *Police Roadblock Operations.* Springfield, Thomas, 1962.

Scott, Walter R. *Fingerprint Mechanics.* Springfield, Thomas, 1951.

Scott, Clifford L., and Garrett, Bill. *Leadership for the Police Supervisor.* Springfield, Thomas, 1960.

Sellin, Thorston, and Wolfgang, Marvin E. *The Measurement of Delinquency.* New York, John Wiley & Sons, 1964.

Short, James F., Jr., and Strodbeck, Fred L. *Group Process and Gang Delinquency.* Chicago, U. of Chicago, 1964.

Stratton, John R., and Terry, Robert M. *Prevention of Delinquency.* New York, MacMillan, 1968.

Sutherland, Edwin H. *Criminology.* Philadelphia, J. B. Lippincott, 1924.

Taft, Donald R. *Criminology.* New York, MacMillan, 1943.

Thorndyke, E. E. *Your City.* New York, Harcourt, Brace, 1939.

VANDERBOSCH, CHARLES C. *Criminal Investigation*. Washington, Professional Standards Div., Int. Assoc. of Chiefs of Police, 1968.

VEDDER, CLYDE B. *Juvenile Offenders*. Springfield, Thomas, 1969.

VOLLMER, AUGUST. *Community Coordination*. Coordinating Councils, 1939.

———*The Police and Modern Society*. Berkeley, U. of California, 1936.

WHEELER, STANTON. *Controlling Delinquency*. New York, John Wiley & Sons, 1968.

WILSON, O. W. *Police Administration*, 2nd ed., New York, McGraw-Hill, 1963.

———*Police Records and Their Installation*. Chicago, Public Administration Service, 1951.

———*Police Planning*, 2nd ed., Springfield, Thomas, 1958.

INDEX